About the author

Lisa Lloyd, known as 'ASD with a G&T', is a fun-loving mum of two neurodivergent children from Kent. As a content creator and co-founder of SEND Reform England, she uses humour and honesty to raise awareness of hidden disabilities. Passionate about sharing the realities of parenting neurodivergent kids who don't fit the mould, Lisa offers support and community to those on a similar journey. Follow Lisa on Instagram, Facebook or TikTok.

Raising the
SEN
~~in~~betweeners

Raising the SEN ~~inbetweeners~~

An honest guide to parenting the kids who fall between the gaps

Lisa Lloyd

Vermilion
LONDON

Vermilion, an imprint of Ebury Publishing

UK | USA | Canada | Ireland | Australia
India | New Zealand | South Africa

Vermilion is part of the Penguin Random House group of companies
whose addresses can be found at global.penguinrandomhouse.com

Penguin Random House UK
One Embassy Gardens, 8 Viaduct Gardens, London SW11 7BW

penguin.co.uk
global.penguinrandomhouse.com

First published by Lisa Lloyd and Amazon in 2024
This edition published by Vermilion in 2025
1

Typeset in 10/16 pt Madera by Jouve (UK), Milton Keynes
Printed and bound in Great Britain by Clays Ltd, Elcograf S.p.A.

The authorised representative in the EEA is Penguin Random House
Ireland, Morrison Chambers, 32 Nassau Street, Dublin D02 YH68

A CIP catalogue record for this book is available from the British Library

ISBN 9781785045882

MIX
Paper | Supporting
responsible forestry
FSC® C018179

Penguin Random House is committed to a sustainable future
for our business, our readers and our planet. This book is made
from Forest Stewardship Council® certified paper.

Dedicating this book to every SEN parent or carer who has fought, and continues to fight, for acceptance and understanding in the face of daily ignorance. I see every single one of you, and your beautiful, incredible children, who make the world a better place.

Too severe for mainstream

Too severe for mainstream,
Not severe enough for SEN school.
Don't help them when they're failing,
Don't catch them when they fall.

They're in a million pieces
When they hit the ground.
Too much damage has been done;
Some pieces can't be found.

So, what becomes of the children,
The ones who are in between?
Forced into mainstream classes,
But rarely ever seen.

The ones left out in corridors
Or put in rooms alone.
The ones who make it there at all,
As many can't leave home.

The noise and the rules
Prove too much for some,
But no one cares about problems
That don't disrupt anyone.

Stuck in a system
That is clearly out of date.
A child with disabilities
Must just accept their fate.

'We are inclusive here,' they say,
But the rules can't be amended.
If you step out of line because of your needs,
Sadly, you will be suspended.

There's no special treatment here;
Everyone's treated the same.
Your autism isn't an excuse, you know –
It's your attitude that's to blame.

And the world wonders why
Mental health problems are on the rise.
Because children are forced to go through school,
Hiding behind a disguise.

Never allowed to show who they are,
Keeping struggles hidden within.
Putting academics above well-being
Is where the problems begin.

School strips our kids of hopes and dreams,
Of being big believers.
The hardship of hidden disability –
No one understands the SEN-Betweeners.

Contents

INTRODUCTION

If you have purchased this book, I imagine it's because you have an autistic child. Or maybe your friend does? Maybe you are a teacher? Maybe you are neurodivergent yourself? Whoever you are . . . thank you for being here. And if you are looking for something a bit sexy . . . I'm sorry but you are lost. There is nothing sexy about this story, I promise you.

Alternatively . . .

What this story is, however, is honest and raw. You could think of it as a journal of my life so far, raising autistic children, in particularly, the in-between children.

Firstly, I guess I should introduce myself. I'm Lisa. I don't usually get to say my own name, so this feels like a bit of a treat. To most people, I'm simply Finley or Poppy's mum, but I'm still an actual person – though I do have to remind myself of that sometimes.

What can I say about myself? I'm a content creator – God, I hate saying that; it sounds so twatty – but this is where my main income comes from now, so that's what I am. I run social media pages called ASD with a G&T.

I would like to think my following has grown because I help others by creating relatable content about autism, but I am not so sure. It could be that I am just a pillock who can't dance, and for some reason, people enjoying watching that. I actually started social media properly when I broke my foot and couldn't get around. I started talking about my life, and a lot about autism and realised there are many people out there in the same position as me:

Completely fucking lost.

In the world of parenting, you soon realise that parenting autistic children is very different, and the rule book goes out the window. I mean, I am totally guessing there is a rule book for neurotypical kids, but in all honesty, I don't know as I have never raised one.

Anyway, this leads me on to introducing the ones that have flipped my world upside down. The real stars of the show.

The one who came into this world angry from the minute he was here (literally crying as his head was out of my hoo-haa, but his body wasn't) is my boy, Finley. Fin is 11 now, though you could mistake him for a 15-year-old as he is so tall. He is intelligent and teaches me things all the time, especially about the natural world. A follower of rules, often very serious but also has a great sense of humour, with a lot of sarcasm. No idea where he gets this from. I blame his father.

And then we have Poppy, our very own Rapunzel who absolutely hates her long hair. The wild child. Poppy is seven, head strong with an incredible imagination. She believes the rules were made to be broken, or better, completely ignored.

Both autistic and both complete opposites.

If you also have autistic children, you have possibly heard 'they don't look autistic' or 'they seem fine to me'.

Maybe you have been told 'they must have mild autism' or the old favourite 'everyone's a little autistic'.

Having two autistic children, I have heard this too often and even from teachers, so I have wondered over the years why people say this – surely not everyone is a dick . . . I don't think.

No, surely not.

I have come up with some conclusions.

- The media is to blame for a lot. We have grown up with films like *Rain Man* showing non-verbal autism but picturing them all as geniuses. Don't get me wrong, *Rain Man*, in my opinion, was an incredible film and from watching that film, I learned about autism for the first time. But it did portray to many people that autism is like that, and only like that.

- People don't understand that many autistic people can 'mask'; that is, cover up their autistic traits to appear neurotypical and blend in. People think of the spectrum as mild to severe, much like as on a scale. From one to ten, how autistic are you? A one? Oh, you are fine then. Just a touch of the 'tism.

- People see autism as a negative, so they feel that saying they don't look autistic is being kind when in fact, it's just telling us that we are going crazy.

- Like I said earlier, some people are just dicks.

The problem is, when you hear this over and over, you start to actually doubt yourself. Maybe they are not autistic = maybe they just really love routines! . . . and flapping . . . and hate eye contact . . . Maybe, I actually tricked all the professionals somehow into believing they were autistic too. Maybe, I am the one going crazy and they are fine. But why would I do such a thing? Why would I try to fool everyone into thinking they are autistic?

Even our children will try and fool us. They will suddenly have a good day. They will interact lots and even give eye contact. They will try new things, even nibble on a bit of cheese off my plate and you will ask yourself was it possibly just a phase? Did I overreact? Then the next day will come with a very different energy. The soul-destroying meltdowns will start, and you think yep, there it is. Definitely autistic still.

To be honest, I'm sure they do it to fuck with us. They have done this to me so many times at the doctors. At home they are near death's door. They have been ill for days and don't show any signs of getting better. I remember one time Poppy didn't eat for days, she just laid on the sofa lifeless (which wasn't like her at all), so I booked an emergency doctor's appointment and explained the situation down the phone to them. They managed to book us in for an appointment in an hour's time. Now anyone that goes to a GP in England will know this is literally unheard of, in fact you may be wondering if you picked up a fiction book while reading this now, but I assure you, this happened.

So, we headed to our extreme emergency appointment, me carrying a very quiet and sleepy Poppy with me, thinking she might end up in hospital for some time.

Literally as we stepped through the doors to the waiting room, something took over Poppy and she was possessed by the spirit of a really well child. The most fucking healthy child you could ever meet.

She was suddenly running up and down the corridor, making the patients laugh. They thought they were just coming to see their GP; they weren't expecting to get a bloody show as well. She was hanging off the arm of a chair as if she were some kind of deranged acrobat that had been locked away for the last five years.

As I am considering leaving, we are called into the doctor's room and I slowly and sullenly drag my child, who is now acting like a gorilla on speed into the room with me. I instantly begin explaining that she was not like this five minutes ago, she really was at death's door, while the doctor stares blankly at me, judging me for this waste of emergency time. So, like I say, I am pretty sure they do this to just screw us over sometimes.

Anyway, this is skipping massively ahead to the actual diagnosis, which we know can take years – if you are lucky. Some kids sadly go through their whole school life struggling, being told they are naughty, stupid or simply being ignored as being incapable and disruptive.

Looking back now, I was one of those. The one who bunked most of school and was caught many times having a fag in the woods behind the school gates. I am ashamed to say that I was disruptive in class and answered back to teachers, but I really didn't want to be that way. I was depressed at such a young age wondering why I didn't fit in anywhere, so I think the acting out was a mask, so no one really knew how I felt.

It all makes sense now. Or does it? I'm pretty sure I'm neurodivergent in some way. I definitely have traits of autism – feeling uneasy with change, getting over-whelmed with people and places – but I also have traits of ADHD – barely ever finishing anything as I get too distracted. (So, if you are reading this, it means I have finished this book, which is pretty unbelievable. Don't ask me how long it took though; I'm guessing I'm probably in my 80s now.)

In fact, I will tell you when I have started writing this. Right now, I am on a plane with the hubby – Terry – and the kids, coming back from our first holiday abroad with them. We did it! We took them out of their routine, out of their comfort zone and it has actually given me a little boost to start writing.

'What an odd time to start writing!' you may say, but as you are probably aware, raising autistic children means you have very little time to yourself. If you find a moment of calm when the kids are occupied, you take that moment. So, I did. Sitting on our easyJet flight, both kids with their headphones in playing a game on their tablets. This is the first time during the entire holiday that we have all sat down quietly, and of course it's on the journey home. The joke of it all is I packed a couple of books with us as I pictured reading them on a sun lounger. Haaa. I had forgotten that I have children and of course I will never get to read a book on a sun lounger again. Those days are long gone.

Starting my book, I asked myself what I would have liked at the beginning of this journey. I read a lot of amazing books on autism, serious ones and funny ones, but none really fit my children. I needed books about navigating mainstream school, fighting for support and learning to ignore people's judgement. I needed books about the in-between children. The ones who mask, the ones who are not severe enough for a special educational needs (SEN) school but can't cope with mainstream. The ones who are dismissed too often as people don't see their disability.

All the books I found were about managing children's behaviour and helping them to adapt, but I soon realised I don't want to force them to adapt. I don't want them to hide their funny 'stims'* or pretend they are OK; I don't want them to struggle silently while they fall behind because the world won't give them even a little bit of grace. They don't need to be fixed; it was the rest of the world that needed fixing. The world of judgement, of outdated ways of teaching, of ableism. But how on earth can I raise happy autistic children when the system is completely broken?

Well, the answer is by trial and error. Learning and unlearning. And I have written this book in the hopes that I can pass on some things to you, the reader, so you don't make the same mistakes I have.

But please remember, all children are different. What works for mine may not work for yours. I am no expert here; I wish I was. Things would have been a lot easier, and I would have saved a lot of money on wine.

We can only try our best. Turns out, there is no manual for autism; just some shitty leaflets printed off from Google that the paediatrician gives you.

---

* Stimming often comes with autism and is a way for the person to self-regulate. It will usually involve repetitive movements, but can be verbal too.

In fact, with all the budget cuts, I'm not sure you will even get that anymore. It's probably a QR code taped to the desk.

I can at least promise you this book will be more informative than those, though in fairness, a Spot the Dog book probably is too, so it's not much of a literary flex.

So, anyway, a huge welcome to our life and what I have learned so far on this crazy journey of raising autistic children, the in-betweeners. The SEN-Betweeners.

Haha. Do you see what I did there?

Chapter One

COMPARISON IS THE THIEF OF JOY

If I could go back in time to me as a terrified new mum, I would tell myself: You can't force your kids to be happy, as much as you can't stop meltdowns from happening.

I know it sounds obvious, but I spent a long time tiptoeing around, trying to not trigger an outburst, doing mental, and sometimes physical, gymnastics to avoid anything that might set them off. It's not only exhausting, but an impossible task.

Trust me, no one can live like that. It felt like there was suddenly a little dictator running the house and I was simply the slave, the servant – in fact, it is still like that to be honest. The kids think there is a magic fairy running around picking up their shoes, making their food, and don't even get me started on flushing the toilet. I just want one day that I look into the toilet bowl and there isn't a massive turd staring back at me. Just one day.

Jokes aside, when Fin was young, I was actually scared what mood he would wake up in and I knew that even if he woke up happy (which was rare), if something triggered him, that would be it for the rest of the day. I remember going into his room and hearing the moaning instantly. I would get a sick feeling in my stomach knowing I had to face the day ahead trying to pacify him, often to no avail.

I wish I had understood that we, as parents, can't put this pressure on ourselves to make our autistic children happy all the time. I wish someone had drummed this into me in the beginning, because I made myself miserable trying to make the most grumpy, serious baby smile and laugh, when really, I should have just given myself a break.

Someone once said to me 'you are only ever as happy as your unhappiest child' and it's so true. I didn't just live with my anxiety; I was my anxiety. I remember looking at other mums ignoring their babies cries and wondering how they did it. They would go about their shopping and carry on like nothing was happening; it wasn't even my baby, but the cry was making me feel on edge. A very unhappy baby and a mum who has anxiety from babies crying was not a good combination, I can tell you that.

I will take you back to six-month-old Fin, for example. We decided to get a baby photoshoot done. I really wanted a newborn one done but all he did was scream, so one month turned into two, until it was soon six months, and I realised this screaming wasn't going away, so sod it, we will go for it anyway.

I used to gaze at people's newborn pictures on social media with envy. All these gorgeous babies fast asleep put into different positions, one looking like he's in a tractor, then flying a plane, the next in a basket cuddling a bear . . . and still fast asleep. How?! Are they drugging these babies? Mine won't even sleep being rocked for hours in a dark room, with a bottle in his mouth, and then we have these other babies, who haven't even stirred while bloody bungee jumping. This is some kind of sick joke! And the mums too! They all look glowing and content in the photos, the perfect picture capturing fierce motherhood in all its beauty. That's definitely not the effect my photo would have on people, mine would give more Worzel Gummidge meets the *Night of the Living Dead* kind of vibes.

So, anyway, we thought it would be a nice idea to have this done when he was around six months, but it didn't go to plan. It rarely does, as Fin had other ideas. He immediately freaked out in the studio – the second the noise of the first camera click went off, he was hysterical and wouldn't calm down. Yep, we hadn't even got one picture, and it was already a disaster. This should have set off alarm bells – why would a baby react so strongly to a camera click? But it was our first baby, and with the first, everything seems abnormal. All babies are utterly unreasonable mini dictators; how do you know when it's too much? We tried rocking, a bottle, a dummy, but he wasn't having any of it. Luckily, the photographer made the decision that we needed to take him outside to calm him, so we changed the location.

The ten-minute car journey to a pretty field relaxed him. We could at least always rely on the car to do this, until the car stopped. I remember the fear of the traffic lights turning red as we had just settled him to sleep. We would creep up the pace of a snail, praying it would turn green by the time we reached it. 'Damn you to hell!' I would silently scream, pleading with desperate eyes as the light seemingly mocked me, staying red slightly longer than usual.

Getting back to the day of the photoshoot, by the time we reached the field, he seemed relaxed, but it still took hours and hours of us jumping around like maniacs pulling silly faces . . . everything we could possibly think of to get one tiny little smirk. And he barely gave us that. In fact, I think he was actually looking down on us in absolute pity and disappointment the whole time at how desperately pathetic we were.

Of course, it all makes sense now. Hindsight is a beautiful thing. The bright lights, a strange person staring and talking to him, the noise. It was sensory overload*, and he was having a meltdown. If only I knew then what I know now. I think I have said this sentence to myself at least one hundred times over the years. At the time, I was so disheartened. All I wanted was some nice pictures of him. Why couldn't he be like the other babies? But by other babies I meant happy, smiling babies. It would have saved us all a lot of time if we had just got natural pictures of him looking serious, just being . . . him. I don't really know who I wanted these pictures for as it would never be true to Fin anyway if he was smiling in them. I think I wanted them so I could believe we were just like all the other families.

It's funny how social media can trick you into believing happiness is in a smile and the perfect life is a rich one. I think some of the saddest people on this earth are the ones hiding behind a smile. But when he was young, these were the pictures I would upload. I would share the one smile of the day, but I wouldn't show the tears surrounding that one photo. I wanted to show people he was happy, if I could prove to others that he was happy and 'normal', maybe I would start believing I wasn't such a shit mum.

---

* Autism quite often comes with sensory issues and my two can often get overwhelmed from sights, smells, noise and other sensations.

I think a lot of what caused my postnatal depression was me feeling like I had done something wrong. I must be a terrible mum. What kind of mum can't comfort her baby?

I found a way that would settle him the most and it was to either strip most of his clothes off and lay him on the floor, or to wiggle him on a cushion. The one thing that most definitely wouldn't comfort him was holding him. This challenged everything I had ever learned about being a mother and caring for a baby.

I raised my concerns with the doctors, as I did start to feel like something was going on, but we were told it was just colic and silent reflux, with both children. I now think otherwise.

I feel it was sensory issues, especially with Poppy. She refused to drink her milk. We tried everything. Dairy free, gluten free, colic meds, I would have tried whisky to be honest if it calmed her, as desperation was setting in with her losing weight, but nothing worked. And her eating problems have continued since. If it's not a chicken nugget and a waffle, she's not interested.

Because of these sensory issues, it caused the babies to cry . . . a lot. People say all babies do is sleep and eat. Well, mine did neither. They just cried. This added to my already terrible anxiety, so every time they cried, it would trigger me, even when Fin became a toddler. I think I am one of the very rare mums that was actually slimmer after giving birth, than before I got pregnant, thanks to the depression and not eating. It's cheaper than Weight Watchers, but I definitely wouldn't recommend it.

All the things that other kids loved, Fin hated. At baby group, the other parents would always know if we were coming, as they would hear his screams before we even got in the room. I just couldn't understand it. Why were all the other kids happy? They would sing, dance, play. Mine was acting like I had strapped him to some kind of bloody torture device when, in fact, we were just singing 'old Macdonald had a farm'. I know my singing is bad but come on.

But I continued to take him there weekly. Why? I have no fucking idea. Maybe because I just didn't know what else to do; babies go to baby groups, so we went. I'm pretty sure it's not because I was enjoying myself. Sitting in a circle singing nursery rhymes while your toddler runs off and ignores you, making you look like a weirdo who comes along to baby groups without a child just for fun is really not my idea of a fun day out.

As much as we both didn't particularly enjoy those groups, I do look back at them with fond memories now and believe they helped me to figure out that Fin was different from his peers. It is sad that so many baby groups are shutting now, when they probably stop so many parents from being lonely. Not that I made many friends from them though, it wasn't easy to with a child screaming in your ear the whole time.

This then began happening everywhere else too, not just baby group. People's houses, parties, days out. He would have huge meltdowns that would sometimes continue until we left the place. I felt resentful in all honesty. This was not how I had pictured having a child would be. How dare he steal my imaginary perfect dream child from me?

A lot of us have grand ideas of no TV and only healthy home cooked meals before having kids. Pah.

We are all perfect parents until we realise how much

fucking hard work it is. But the one thing I thought I could be sure of was he would enjoy a farm. All kids enjoy farms, don't they? I used to watch kids TV; they were always visiting the farm. Kids love that shit.

Apparently not.

Every time we stepped into a barn area he would scream the place down. It clicked eventually; it was the farmyard smell. Again, another sensory issue. Family would laugh at us when we tried to tell them that he goes mental if you take him into a barn. They said it must be a coincidence, but I knew it was the smell as it happened every single time.

OK, so that's farms off the list. Swimming? Nope. Getting changed was too much of a nightmare. Soft play? Too noisy. Friends' houses? Nope. Too peopley. Shopping? Too . . . I have no idea to be honest, but he fucking hated it. And this is how we carried on – taking my miserable child out and being miserable myself. Until I snapped.

It was my cousin's 18th birthday party. All the family were there. There was music and lights; basically, a sensory overload. Fin wanted to take a cereal packet with him. I'm not sure why, but sometimes we just do whatever to make life easier, so we took an empty pack of Cheerios with us. Since having Poppy, I am very used to taking random objects around with us. Many times, I have had to carry garden ornaments on our days out. (I'm not talking about small ones either – massive decorative plant pots that weigh a ton.) And tiny objects that we are constantly at risk of losing, such as the dead fly we had to take to school. Yes, we really did. The poor teachers look terrified sometimes with what Poppy is going to hand them. So, this is now quite the norm for us, but it wasn't back when Fin was young.

This was around the time I started to notice the stares. I could see people wondering why my boy was carrying a cereal box around with him. I felt judged so I took it and replaced it with his postman pat van toy. Luckily, he let me do this but, in turn, became fixated with the toy. He wouldn't engage with anyone or look at anyone; he just laid on the floor rolling the van back and forth and spinning the wheels around.

Now I know this was a coping mechanism for him, now I know he was in sensory hell and didn't want to be there. Now . . . now I know.

But I didn't see that then. All I saw was children running around, laughing and dancing, while I stood once again on the outer edge stuck with my child who wouldn't even acknowledge my family. Wouldn't appreciate the party, wouldn't have fun where I thought he should.

So, I did the worst thing I could do. I took it away in temper. In that moment, all I felt was anger. It was built up from years of trying to get him to interact, years of trying to get him to enjoy things the other children did. Years of trying to bond with a child that didn't want cuddles and had no interest in me. I had had enough. I felt defeated. I had failed as a mum. I couldn't even get him to enjoy a family party.

Through tears, I am ashamed to say, I shouted at him and told him he needed to join in. He broke down. We both did that day. I saw the sadness in his face and, worst of all, the fear of me. He didn't understand what he did wrong, because he actually did nothing wrong. It was me; I was in the wrong.

It pains me to write this, as I'm ashamed of myself and

I still feel the guilt to this day, but sometimes it takes the darkest of moments to start to notice the light shining through. This was a turning point for me, one which was sorely needed.

When I was in tears with Fin having a meltdown in my arms, my parents and Terry took him outside. They found a park to take him to. It was night time and pitch black, lit only by Terry's torch on his phone, but Fin was happy again. He found a safe space, away from the noise, and people, and lights, and heat, and this was where he needed to be.

While they were comforting my son and protecting him from my harsh words, I was sat in the party surrounded by people, but feeling completely alone. It felt like a scene in a film, everyone dancing and chatting around me, but it was all blurred and white noise. I wasn't focused on anything except thinking about my child I had just let down. I knew this was no longer where I was meant to be either. I was meant to be with him, my boy.

I had spent the early years of his life so busy looking at others that I was actually missing what was right in front of me. I was missing everything. It's true when they say comparison is the thief of joy. It really is, as it brings nothing but misery.

And this is when I finally let go. I let go of all my ideas of what parenting looked like. I stopped focusing on what he wasn't doing, and chose to celebrate what he was doing. I began to step into his world instead of forcing him, literally kicking and screaming, into ours.

There, standing at the threshold of this new, different, beautiful world, I looked back at my old life for the last time and said a final goodbye to who I used to be before

I became a mum. I said goodbye to the life that was, yes, easier but also empty.

Most importantly, I said goodbye to the ghost of what I thought motherhood and parenting was supposed to be.

I stared at a life before me full of happy stims, chicken nuggets, sensory toys, ear defenders, and tablet time. I stepped forward and I never looked back again.

Top Tips

☆ *Most importantly, stop blaming yourself for everything your child can't do. If you do not take credit for everything they have achieved, then you can't feel responsible for all the things they are behind with.*

☆ *Stop comparing. Every child takes their own time to do things. This isn't a race and the only person you're competing with is yourself.*

☆ *It is impossible to keep your children happy 24/7, so stop trying to achieve the impossible. Accept the fact that sometimes they will feel sad, sometimes they will have meltdowns to express how they feel and that is OK. No one is happy 100 per cent of the time, and children aren't any different.*

Chapter Two

THE DIAGNOSIS

Once I accepted that Fin was different, I began researching. When I say researching, I mean googling. I know everyone says it's the last thing you should do, and I usually agree. Yes, I have looked up a mosquito bite before and it's basically said I have two weeks to live, so I agree, Google is not always great for diagnosing symptoms. Yet sometimes it is when you are not really sure what you are looking for.

I couldn't go to the doctors; he wasn't ill. And when I spoke to friends and family, I was met with the same responses: 'He's just a boy,' 'He will grow out of it,' 'You're worrying too much.' How can you go to the doctors to say, 'My child is really anxious with people, and screams if he gets wet, and hates hugging me'? It would be such an odd thing to go to the doctor about and I imagined I would be met with the response simply being that he is a child, and I am wasting their time.

The thing was as well, he was hitting his milestones – advanced in fact. He was obsessed with letters and numbers, and I proudly showed videos on Facebook showing him reciting the alphabet around the age of one. Yes, I was one of those mums, I'm sorry.

Hear me out: My child barely smiled, so I needed to gloat about something. I needed a win. Sue me.

We couldn't believe we had raised such a genius child. He was fascinated by the alphabet, and it would be something that would keep him happy most of the time. He was enriched by CBeebies and the inestimable Alphablocks. Some of the finest alphabet-based television I've ever seen. It was fun followed up by the hit sequel, Numberblocks. Genius. Where do they come up with this stuff?

There was also Numberjacks, but I think he had a bit of a love/hate relationship with that. I get it though; it was creepy as fuck.

So, I spent my days scrolling through NHS websites, mum chat groups, and social media. I searched for high-maintenance children (it seems a strange term to use, I know, but I couldn't search 'babies acting like arseholes'), serious babies, fussy toddlers, obsessions, repetitive behaviours, fussy eating, and overly sensitive. I actually drove myself mad searching over and over. I just needed some answers to know that I wasn't going mad.

And the more I searched, the more I kept coming back to the same result: autism. But how could it be autism? Autism wasn't supposed to be like this. He speaks, he makes eye contact, and he can't count how many matchsticks I just threw on the floor. He's not *Rain Man*.

Yes, this is embarrassingly the way I thought. But as far as I was concerned, I had never met an autistic person in my life. This is hilarious now as I believe many of the people I've been surrounded by my whole life are neurodivergent – but that's for another story.

So, I took my findings to Terry, who immediately dismissed me. He knew I had been struggling with Fin and believed I was just looking for an answer as to why he was so much hard work, which to be fair, is exactly what I was doing.

Like me, he only knew the stereotypes about autism and that was it, so he wouldn't have it. He would say that autism is a disability. Our child isn't disabled. You are just depressed and overthinking it. I mean, I was, but that didn't mean Fin wasn't autistic.

The problem was, Terry hadn't been around other children Fin's age, so he had nothing to compare to. Being our first child, he just assumed this is what all kids do.

'All kids scream when the hand dryers go off.'

Maybe some do, but do they have a huge meltdown and refuse to go back in the toilets ever again?

'All kids get shy sometimes.'

Again, yes, but they are not terrified of someone saying hello to the point of being sick. Family members don't have to look away every time they meet in case the eye contact sends them into hysterics.

'All kids dislike the feeling of wet clothes. I don't like sitting there in wet clothes.'

OK but do they have to strip off completely naked if one drop lands on their T-shirt from their drink, screaming at the same time?

And this is how our arguments went on for some time, and these are the arguments I still have with people now. I use this example quite often to people. Everybody goes for a wee, weeing is a perfectly normal human behaviour, but if you were to pee 20 times within an hour, there could be a problem there as that is not the norm.

Again and again, I would try to explain the differences, but Terry is naturally a very suspicious person. He needs hard evidence to believe things, but this is the issue with autism and the reason it is called a hidden disability. It is not obvious sometimes, it is difficult to quantify, so he continued to believe I was overreacting and just reading into things. Until he finally saw for himself.

We decided to go to Terry's friend's house for the day, their girl was a similar age, and we stupidly thought maybe they could play together.

I mean, I say 'we', but Terry thought this. I knew what would happen, as it had happened at my friend's house a few weeks before, so I was feeling on edge before we had even left. I definitely knew he wouldn't play with their child; he didn't seem to even like other children and would ignore them most of the time. As much as I tried to get him to join in and say hello, he never would.

As always, I packed all the toys I could think of that I would wave ineffectually to try to keep him happy; I honestly looked like I was going on holiday everywhere I went. This wasn't your average baby bag. On top of the baby bag we had cuddly toys, building blocks, a tablet obviously, a change of clothes, a random object that he has become fixated with – usually a rock, books, light up toys, a ball. Honestly, I looked like the old junk lady out of *The Labyrinth*, weighed down by all his shit I had to take everywhere. 'What's the matter, my dear? Don't you like your toys?'

When we finally arrived, he was already starting to moan. The car had stopped, and you have to be out of it in 0.2 seconds or he will throw a fit. We also had a problem if he fell asleep in the car going to a new place. Many times, he would fall asleep, and we would have to sit and wait for him to wake up. Honestly, it would take hours sometimes but if we woke him, he would be hysterical. We would also have to wait for him to adjust. We couldn't just get him out of the car the second he woke, we would have to sit and let him slowly get used to his surroundings. This is why I say it is exhausting raising children with additional needs as everything takes longer.

This eventually becomes your norm though and you forget that other people don't have to do this every time they go out in the car.

Even us just approaching the door filled me with dread. I was so sure that every time he had a meltdown it was a reflection on me. I felt like people were wondering: 'Why is her child so miserable all the time, it must be her parenting. What a terrible mother.'

I also desperately wanted people to like him. I wanted them to see his occasional smile and his funny little mannerisms. I wanted them to hear his little voice and see how gentle he was, but no one saw that side. They just saw the inconsolable screaming baby. And that's exactly what he was again. We had barely said hello and Fin had switched into meltdown mode. My heart sank.

He was thrashing around, hyperventilating, sweat dripping off him from getting so worked up. The only thing we could do to try to calm him was take him away from them into the garden. This usually would help, but even this didn't work. We were torn about what to do. Do we push through in the hopes he will one day adjust? Are we being rude to our friends if we just leave? Is he just playing up to get his own way? Did we maybe not let him interact with enough people when he was a baby? Should one of us leave with him while the other stays? But then we would have to travel back again with him to pick them up, causing him more distress. All of these questions were running through my mind while I also tried to appear calm and happy to our friends, maintaining the mask of happiness when really inside I just wanted to break down and scream that I had had enough. But I didn't, and I said what I always said: 'Maybe we should go. He is a bit tired today. I think he might be coming down with something.' And that was it; we decided there was no comforting him, so we left.

As we drove back in the car, Terry turned to me and said the words I had been longing to hear. 'I see what you mean, this isn't right. I think we need to get him seen by a doctor.'

Finally, he understood this wasn't just a toddler crying. This was so extreme and something you could only truly understand by seeing it for yourself. There was something else going on and by this stage, I knew in my heart it was autism.

The next day, I phoned the health visitor and said I needed them to assess him, and they arranged an appointment with me. Of course, they wanted to come to the house, and I went into mad mum cleaning mode. Throwing everything I owned into our bedroom. Even to this day when people visit us, that place is where all our junk, unsorted clothes, random garbage and mess goes, so we can pretend we don't live like animals. It is our room of shame. No one must enter there.

I cleaned like I had never cleaned before, because obviously they would blame our untidy house as the reason our child is autistic. Didn't you know that you, the lazy mother who has not cleaned behind her fridge in five years, have caused your child to be touched by the 'tisms? For shame!

In fact, the health visitor turned out to be lovely and said she could definitely see some traits. I asked her if she thought it was autism, but she said she couldn't answer that. I understood she couldn't make those claims, but I so longed for confirmation that I wasn't going crazy.

Though I definitely did start to go crazy while waiting for the diagnosis. It doesn't sound like a hard thing, just waiting, but in reality, it feels like you are completely lost and alone. You are raising a child with a disability, but no one is aware.

That is so bloody tough. You are watching the other children gain confidence while your child is losing theirs. You see their social skills improving and watch them turn into little people, while yours is kind of . . . stuck. Someone once said to me it is like being in the toddler stage forever and I understood that feeling. It felt like we were always taking one step forward but two steps back. You must just watch, helplessly, as they fall further and further behind and there is nothing you can do but wait.

So, in the end, I thought fuck that. So, I started telling people. If he got upset with people talking to him at the park, I would simply explain: 'He's autistic and won't reply to you.' Some people don't agree with doing this before a diagnosis, but I believe as a parent you know. And let's not forget, you are still raising an autistic child before they get that diagnosis – they don't just suddenly become autistic after your appointment. Trust your instinct as it's usually right. Telling people helped me. It helped me change my parenting and teaching to adapt to him more.

I had to believe he was autistic to do that otherwise we were stuck in limbo, and I would be parenting him incorrectly. For example, if I were to treat him as a neurotypical child, I would therefore be telling him off for things that he literally can't help. I would be putting him in situations that would make him distressed and uncomfortable. So, the only way I could do it right was by assuming he was already autistic and parenting that way, I felt that to dismiss his needs before getting that bit of paper with a diagnosis on it would have been far crueller.

Though on the odd occasion, parents can get it wrong. Like I did when Poppy came along. Poppy was actually worse than Fin as a baby.

Let's all just let that sink in for a second.

Yep, I didn't think this was possible, but it was. During the pregnancy with her, my friends and family all reassured me and said I wouldn't have another newborn like Fin, screaming constantly with colic.

Ha, what a terrible joke! Never tell me the universe is without a sense of humour, sick and twisted though it may be. I certainly felt like someone was taking the piss out of me.

Poppy made Fin look like an easy baby. You see, the problem with Poppy was not that she would just scream after feeding, it was that she wouldn't feed at all.

She would drink a tiny bit and then begin screaming in what sounded like agony, which would then turn into a hunger cry. And this is how the cycle went on. I can't even begin to tell you the feeling it gave to know your baby was hungry but couldn't eat. I think we all know the type of hungry cry newborns give when they need to feed and to hear it constantly was soul destroying.

The depression came back again and not just me this time, it hit Terry too. We were both eaten up with guilt to Fin feeling like we had disrupted his whole little world. We were still going through the process of getting Fin diagnosed and not only did Fin have his world changed with a new baby coming along (which is a pretty big change), but with one that screamed nonstop and would trigger his meltdowns from the noise. Worse, I couldn't comfort him properly as I was too busy trying to stop Poppy from crying and getting her to eat.

No one was sleeping or eating, and we were finding it hard to parent Fin at all as we were constantly trying to console Poppy. People talk about the love that a baby brings into a home; but not this home. It really was the most miserable house you had ever seen. We were all just existing at this point and trying to survive. I kept trying to tell myself it would get better as it had with Fin, but it was hard to see the light at the end of the tunnel when you are in the thick of it.

I hope no one is reading this that hasn't had kids yet, as I imagine this will put you off for life. Actually, maybe they should hand this book out to teens at school as a form of contraception.

Jokes aside, not all babies are like this, I promise. I think. I mean, I don't know, I am just assuming otherwise, why do people go on to have more?

I just seem to have a natural talent for making miserable newborns. I always wanted to have a skill but I'm not too pleased with this one if I'm honest. Something less traumatic would be nice, like being able to sing maybe.

It all came to a head one day; Poppy was losing weight, and we were terrified. I was tired of trying different milks and bottles that the doctor suggested. We had tried so many; anti-colic, lactose free, wheat free, air free, taste free, you name it we tried it.

So, I made the decision to take her to A and E. I didn't know what else to do. I drove there in a blur, her screaming in the car seat next to me leaving Terry and Fin at home to get some peace. I walked through the reception, exhausted with tears streaming down my face, carrying her screaming in my arms. I could feel everyone staring and, of course, why wouldn't they? This wasn't a little whimper – this was a blood-curdling scream like she was on fire. I walked up to the reception desk and simply handed my baby over to the stranger at the desk. I said I can't do this anymore.

This was without a shadow of a doubt the lowest point of my life. I handed my child over to a person I had never met before, and at that moment, I wanted to walk out and leave and never come back. I had lost all hope and was at breaking point. It worries me to think about what could have happened that night if I hadn't gone to A and E. I am sure I would have never hurt her, but I was having very dark thoughts about myself.

But thankfully, the reception and nurses were incredible, they told me to step outside and take a break. I sat out there for a while smoking. It helped to just step away, it helped to tell someone I wasn't coping. I don't know how long I was out there for, but I remember looking at my hands shaking in front of me. After some time, I eventually went back in and faced my reality. I saw the doctor and he suggested weaning Poppy early. She was barely three months and couldn't sit up so I was a little shocked, but he told me that if we didn't and she kept dropping weight, she would be tube fed. We had tried everything else, so I was willing to give it a go and like some kind of miracle, it only bloody worked, pretty much instantly.

We fed her mushed porridge and some banana, and the next morning we woke up to a smiling, happy baby. I am honestly not exaggerating; it was like someone had handed us a different child. I was almost too scared to believe it and didn't want to enjoy it too much, in case it all came crashing down and stopped, breaking me once again. But it didn't.

She started to gain weight, and she was the happiest little baby. She smiled back at us which is something I wasn't used to with Fin. She was actually responding to our smiles and laughs. As she got a little older, she pointed and clapped. This was so strange to me; she was actually interacting with not only us but strangers too. People in the shops would say hello to her and she would actually smile at them. I know this doesn't sound like a big deal, but to us it was huge. I had spent three years prior to this terrified of anyone looking at my child in case it set off a meltdown and now my daughter is waving at strangers! I wanted to shout it from the rooftops!

And one of the things that had been playing on our minds prior to having Poppy was the obvious question when your first has been referred for autism ... 'Will my second be autistic too?' And at this stage we had decided she 100 per cent wasn't following in her brother's footsteps. She was so social and happy. The complete opposite to Fin. Of course, she isn't autistic.

Until around the age of one. Once again, the same feelings started occurring that Poppy was a little different to her peers, but I just told myself, everyone's a little weird – her parents especially – she is just quirky. I also started to notice some flapping. After reading so much about autism with Fin, I knew it was common for autistic children to flap their arms with excitement, which is exactly what Poppy was doing, but I didn't take too much notice because it was something that Fin had never done. They were still so different, even with reaching milestones. Poppy was a late walker and started around 18 months whereas Fin was walking around the age of one. In fact, Fin followed the rules even with reaching milestones in typical Fin fashion. He even arrived on his due date. Of course he did. They said we were expecting him on June 30th, so that is exactly when he decided to arrive – rules are rules of course. There's a timetable people!

Poppy, however, was not moving for anyone. She was two weeks overdue and had to be induced. I feel like the PDA traits were obviously there already in the womb, people were telling her she needed to leave, and she was like fuck that and fuck you. I'm staying and you can't force me to leave.

As time went on, we started to notice more traits. Once she was finally walking, she would sometimes tiptoe walk, and it would usually be when she was distressed. We then realised she wasn't responding to her name when we called her, and actually couldn't reach her at all at times. It was like she had disappeared somewhere and was no longer in the room with us. Only her body remained as an anchor to this reality.

I'm not going to lie. My heart sank a little as I thought 'here we go again'. And trust me, that is when you really start to question your parenting. One autistic child could easily be random but two means I am to blame. It was my parenting. Obviously, we now know it's probably in our genes, but I didn't know that then.

The feeling of being upset wasn't so much that she could be autistic, but instead the thought that she would go through all the struggles Fin had and I didn't want that for her. I had seen how he couldn't cope in busy settings and how hard it was to get a diagnosis as we were still waiting for his. I had heard that it was even harder for girls to get a diagnosis, so I began to think it would be impossible. I couldn't stand the thought of her being miserable like Fin had been at school and not being able to do anything about it. All these worries hit me like a ton of bricks and once again, I felt like I had failed my child somehow as I couldn't do anything to make their lives better for them.

Like everyone says though, if you have met one autistic person, you have met one autistic person, and this is so true. Poppy didn't have the same struggles as Fin. She had a whole different set of struggles, which is great fun. It's so much fun in fact that I write this while sobbing into my third glass of wine.

Little did I know that our diagnosis journey would run a lot smoother with Poppy than with Fin. Fin's diagnosis process was an endless task, climbing a mountain and getting knocked back constantly. The biggest problem was him being a huge masker at school, which I will cover in Chapter 3 as that needs a whole section to itself!

Fin actually had three assessments in total. One a year. The first two times we were told we would need to go back again as he was borderline autistic. Yes, apparently that is a thing. I have no idea how though; can you be borderline pregnant? Technically, all of us women are borderline pregnant when we have eggs sitting in us ready to be fertilised . . .

The appointments left me feeling more disheartened every time, as no one was listening, and once again we were left without any support while the system ummed and err'd.

We spent a couple of hours each time running through questions, Fin completed the puzzles they asked him to and once again we were told they couldn't diagnose yet. After four long years, we finally had our last assessment. I was so nervous prior to it. I knew how great Fin was at masking and for the first time ever, I hoped and prayed for a meltdown.

That may sound odd, but I wanted someone to see the real him, the one behind the mask, the one I could see. I wanted them to recognise his struggles. I actually wondered what I could do before the meeting to put him in a bad mood. I realise this sounds awful but when you get this desperate you start to have these thoughts. So, I played really loud drums next to him and made him eat broccoli . . . I'm joking! I am not that bad of a mum; it did cross my mind though.

Instead, I just told him over and over that he could be himself, he wouldn't be in trouble, and he doesn't have to talk to anyone if he is not comfortable to. It sounds like such an obvious thing, but I think it is really important to remind our kids that they will not be in trouble for being who they are, even if they don't wish to speak to anyone. For so long they are taught to step out of their comfort zone and behave a certain way, so I wanted to make sure he knew that he didn't have to pretend that day.

Once we were in there, it took a while for him to talk to them and he hid behind me for the first 15 minutes. Luckily, he began stimming, rocking back and forth from being uncomfortable. I did a little silent 'yes!' in my head. I wanted them to see this. They tried to get him to play with them, but he wouldn't engage until they started talking about his special interest*. As they spoke more about this subject, which I think was Halloween or zombies, he then started to come out of his shell more.

We must have been in there about an hour and a half, and the paediatrician then spoke to me separately and told me that he was diagnosing Fin with Autism Spectrum Disorder, Sensory Processing Disorder and hypermobility. I couldn't believe it. Four years from being referred, six years of having everyone around me tell me that he wasn't. Six years of me trying to tell the world that he wasn't coping, he wasn't rude, he wasn't weird – he was autistic. Six years of waiting for this moment, to be handed this bit of paper. I burst into tears on the spot. He told me how sorry he was, and he can still live a good life with support.

---

* Many autistic people have special interests – anything from an activity to a TV show, to a colour – that can be so intense that the individual doesn't enjoy anything else.

I wiped away my tears and replied, 'No, these are not tears of sadness, they are tears of relief.' And they were. They were tears that had built up for six years of hearing 'he is fine', 'stop trying to label your child', 'he's just shy'. It was the confirmation I had needed all along and I'm so glad I had trusted my gut.

Poppy, on the other hand, had her one and only appointment within a year. Again, she was seen by a health visitor who referred her straight away. The health visitor was trying to get Poppy to engage, but typical Pops was on her own agenda. The health visitor kept handing her items that Poppy would look at in disgust and then immediately throw across the room. So, I guess I understood why she was referred quite early on, but I am still unsure why we were seen so quickly. I believe some of it must have been because she was speech delayed and displayed more 'typical' autistic traits than Fin. A year almost felt quick when, as SEN parents, we are so used to being stuck on the waiting list for years and fighting for any support.

I didn't even feel the need to fight like I did with Fin. Nobody disagreed with me when I told them I thought she was autistic, or that she had been referred for an assessment. I never got the 'she doesn't look autistic' which we heard so many times with Fin. So, whatever autism looks like, Poppy obviously rocks it.

Poppy's appointment was very different to Fin's. They sat observing us 'play' while taking notes. I say play, but it was basically an hour of me trying, thrusting toys in Poppy's face, for her to make me look like an absolute twat and ignore me the whole time. She was also flapping throughout. Turns out that is perfect for an Autism diagnosis as we got it on the spot. I must say, I wasn't as emotional with Poppy's diagnosis as I was with Fin's. I knew what to expect this time, and I didn't feel like I had to prove so much with Poppy, as people could see it for themselves.

I stepped out of the office once again, holding the leaflets that were printed off a Google search about autism, but this time with my little girl's hand in mine. I had been there not so long before with Fin, but it was a different feeling this time, one filled with more confidence, one that reflected my inner thoughts. This time I just knew that somehow, we would be OK. I was ready to throw the leaflets in the bin once we got home because this time, I trusted myself more than the professionals. This time I knew for certain my instincts were right, and no one will ever understand my children better than I can.

Top Tips

☆ *You can ask for a referral of an autism/ADHD diagnosis through your health visitor or GP.*

☆ *Even if you are unsure, I would recommend asking for a referral as the waiting list is years. If you don't feel you need the assessment anymore, you can simply cancel the appointment.*

☆ *If you decide to go private, check that the diagnosis is recognised by the NHS, schools, etc.*

☆ *Write down everything to take to the appointment with you as you will forget things when going there.*

☆ *Take video footage to help the paediatrician to see any autistic traits they may not see during the appointment.*

☆ *Be confident that you know your child better than anyone.*

Chapter Three

ANOTHER BRICK
IN THE WALL*

If you are still waiting for a diagnosis, or your child has recently been diagnosed, you will probably be asking yourself the same question all of us ask after you receive the paperwork confirming autism or ADHD ... What support do we get now? Can't wait to see the wealth of resources I have access to now, right?

I hate to be the one to break it to you, but the answer is none. You receive the medical report on your child and then you are left to skip off into the sunset with your child, holding your very important paperwork and live happily ever after.

At least, that is what would happen in a film. In reality, you are chasing your child across the car park, while clinging on to the paperwork, trying to juggle making sure your child doesn't get run over and eagerly reading through to find the section that says about the support your child will receive, until eventually you realise that section doesn't exist.

The only 'support' that you do get offered is a parenting course, and what fun this is. I made the mistake

---

* A song title by Pink Floyd, written by Roger Waters.

of attending this after we got Fin's diagnosis, bearing in mind that Fin was six years old at the time. That is six years where I had already been parenting prior to the parenting course. The course really needed to be offered about six years ago when I was thrown into becoming a SEN parent without a fucking clue what I was doing. But hey ho, maybe the course had some strategies and tips that I hadn't thought of before. It was based around sensory issues, so I was keen to go.

When I got there, I was shocked to learn that the lady teaching the course didn't have autistic children; in fact, she didn't have children at all. I was dubious but I still gave her the benefit of the doubt and listened to what she said. After she began explaining that some children will struggle with noise and want to cover their ears, I soon knew this was a mistake and a complete waste of time. She didn't even give an answer to the problem, she asked us parents what we suggested – oh don't worry love, we will just run the bloody course for you. She was literally just explaining what autism was to us, the parents that had already been raising autistic children. Unbelievable!

That was 60 minutes of my life I will never get back. As we all know, child-free time is one of the most important things in the world. Never ever make me waste those precious moments, it may cost you your life. I was RAGING.

It was like attending a course at work with your boss telling you how to do the job you have been doing for the last five years.

On top of this shit show of a course, run by the local authorities, I went out to my car and discovered I had got a parking ticket. That was £60 for me to go to a meeting run by someone who knew less about Autism Spectrum Disorder (ASD) than I did. What a joke! I should have charged them for wasting my time!

And that was it for the 'support'. No fucking answers to anything and a parking ticket for my time. Maybe they do this as a way to break you into your life as a SEN parent, giving you really low expectations of support so you can be pathetically grateful for any crumbs of help they might decide to throw you.

You then find out they actually need something called an EHCP to get support at school.

This, as some of you may know, is an Education Health Care Plan. You have to apply to the local authority for this to get them to fund the support for your child. Without this, the school will not be able to meet their needs, and your child will be unable to get into a SEN school. So yeah, it's pretty fucking important. A little heads up would've been good, but whatever.

As I started looking into how to apply, it dawned on me that it's even more paperwork and even more waiting, so off I went to get prepared for my next fight.

I personally believe the EHCP is actually more important than the diagnosis for school. Fin went through preschool and the first few years of primary school without an EHCP and even in that short space of time, damage had already been done.

Fin just about managed preschool. He was always the quiet child but still cried every time I took him in. I guess preschool was never going to be too much of a struggle as it's all play-based learning, but one of the things I did notice him struggling with was the other children.

I noticed early on that the other children were running up greeting each other at the gates, showing each other their new toys, but Fin just stood clinging to me. My heart broke a little every time I turned up. I would whisper to him, pointing out the other children, asking their names or if he wanted to say hello, but he would just continue to hide behind me. I hoped he would make some friends, but it looked like friendships were going to have to be forced through me meeting up with the school mums and, truthfully, I didn't want to speak to the other school mums either.

Is it still a mystery where he gets this anti-social side from?

At the gates, I had mentioned to the teachers about him being referred for autism, but they all said they couldn't see any issues, and this became the same at primary school, even though he was struggling more and more as the years went on.

The first year at primary was nothing but hell on earth to be honest. The meltdowns he had were huge at home, and he spent his days too terrified to speak at school.

Having good teachers can make the biggest difference between kids that love or hate school. Thankfully, we've mostly had amazing teachers but any bad experiences can leave quite an impression on children.

Cutting a very long story short, I spoke to Fin's teacher about it and the Head. This was me immediately making my great first impression as the troublesome mum. I know, I know, this was not exactly going to help my plea for more support for Fin, but I have this terrible compunction to speak up when I see something is not right. I truly believe that any 'old school' teachers need retraining, especially in Special Educational Needs and Disabilities (SEND).

I would try to explain to the teachers and the Head that Fin was having huge meltdowns at home and not coping, but they just kept telling me he was fine in school. Of course, I knew he wasn't fine at all. He was masking and I need a whole other chapter to talk about masking, as unfortunately so many people still don't understand it.

The thing is, I understood Fin's feelings more than anyone as I always hated school, it was one of the worst times of my life.

I think some people are academic and some are not, and if you are not, then school is really tough. Though to be fair, my school was a hell lot worse than Fin's. Terry often refers to my school as the prison school. Sadly, that is how many schools are run: children having to put their hands up to go to the toilet, a uniform that everyone must wear to look the same. Detention for minor things, such as forgetting a bit of equipment to bring with you, no talk-ing, no running, sitting at a desk for hours, grey desks, grey uniforms, minimal breaks. It's pretty sad when you look at it, especially sad when you think that this is how children are spending the majority of their time instead of playing, running and exploring.

Don't get me wrong, school is super important, and I take my hat off to the teachers; in fact, I take my whole outfit off for the teachers. They do one of the hardest, most important and most underpaid jobs: They shape the future for us all.

It's just that a one-size-fits-all way of learning does not, in fact, fit all.

I got a little glimpse of what teachers do during lockdown when we tried to do home learning. I have one thing to say about that: Hell no.

I'm surprised I didn't lose all my hair due to stress. Lockdown made me wonder why I had kids at all. I love my kids to pieces but teaching them and being with them 24/7 is not what I need in my life. I know the feeling is mutual also; Fin told me many times that I was a rubbish teacher.

I remember checking the news daily to see when they would be opening the schools again. The days felt so long. There was nowhere to go and nothing to do.

Lockdown, however, was probably the best time Fin has ever had. He didn't have to leave the house and didn't have to see people – literally his idea of heaven. Poppy was too young to really understand what was going on, but I do feel bad that she missed that year of toddler days out, trips to farms and play groups.

The toddler stage goes so quickly (not when you are in it) and I wanted us to enjoy this time together while Fin was at school, giving Pops the same one-on-one time that Fin had before she was born.

The only place I occasionally took her was Tesco – we all know this became a day out during lockdown – especially since you had to queue down the road to be let in. It was like a theme park, waiting to go on the depressing fruit aisle ride.

Taking an autistic toddler during this time was not for the faint hearted, literally, because everyone was freaking out about everything. People standing with their face mask on, rubbing their hands together with hand gel, staring absolutely horrified at my three-year-old licking the trolley handles.

Unfortunately for me, lockdown happened just before Fin received his EHCP meaning that he wasn't classed as a vulnerable child so I couldn't send him in to school. I was raging inside – he had his diagnosis of autism. Surely there should be some perks of having an autistic child, which would have been he would be one of the children that would still get to go to school. Honestly, what was the point in the diagnosis without the EHCP?

Lockdown was great for the kids like Fin but not so great for my mental health. I wouldn't look back on it as such a hard time if it wasn't for the aftermath of lockdown. Getting the kids (who already struggled socially) to interact with people again and get back into a routine of school again was really, really hard.

Social skills don't come naturally to many autistic children, it's something that must be learned and continually worked on to keep up and improve, but obviously we couldn't during lockdown as you weren't allowed to see people. Well, unless you were invited to a government 'Work Event' (with cheese and wine), of course!

I remember when we first met up with our friends again. My friend's children, Otis and Orla – whom Fin had practically grown up with. When he saw them again it was like they were strangers. He wouldn't interact with them or even look at them, and I knew it was going to take a long time to get him back to feeling comfortable again. Poppy, of course, couldn't give a shit and ran straight up to them like she had been seeing them every day. Then again,

I think she would do that if she'd never seen them before in her life, she's just like that.

The hardest part, though, was going back to school, and the going in was worse than ever. It was like going back after the summer holidays but ten times worse. Don't get me wrong, once they were in school, I was having my own mini party. Champagne flowing, music blaring, me dancing around my empty house, but it was getting them in that was the issue. Fin would beg for me to not send him in, and I would feel like the worst parent in the world.

It was mostly hard for Fin as it was such a contrast from no demands, safe around the house, being naked a lot of the time and stimming constantly, to suddenly the strict school environment again.

I think the reason so many people want SEN schools is because they have a completely different approach to learning, which is better suited to our children. Learning through play, sensory activities, regular movement breaks. I personally feel this should be for every child regardless of whether they have additional needs or not and I know they do this in other countries too. Kids aren't designed to be sat at a desk all day, even adults struggle to. I know I did when I worked in an office. Any excuse and I'd be out of that chair in a heartbeat.

So, year 2 was here and Fin was starting to drop behind academically more and more. He had started off school advanced and now was about a year behind his peers. I knew it was because he wasn't getting the correct support he needed. The Head Teacher and I butted heads quite a few times, and I knew it was because Fin was masking so well when he was at school. But then year 2 hit and the mask started to drop. I honestly don't blame her or the teachers though. I imagine it's incredibly hard to know how to support a child that appears to not need support at all. I even asked the teachers to speak to him privately about how he was feeling. Every time they did, he would just reply that he was fine. So, he kept holding up this mask until it became too heavy, until he literally couldn't hold it anymore and it began to slip. I remember going into the parents evening and the teacher telling me that she was starting to see some of what I was talking about.

This moment would change everything for us.

By this time, the school had now opened an SRP (Specialist Resource Provision) for children with additional needs. This was a very large room, with an outdoor space filled with sensory toys, weighted blankets, blackout tents, sensory lighting and yoga balls. A place that the children could escape to from the class of 32 children and stim, run and let it all out. A place they could finally be themselves, where they could hang their mask up at the door and run free. I knew this was where Fin needed to be.

The school applied for an EHCP for Fin and, of course, the assessment was rejected. The local authority said he basically hadn't failed enough for them to even come and visit him. I remember the meeting I had with the special educational needs co-ordinator (SENCo), and she said he needed to completely fail before they could get any funding for him.

I was so shocked that this is how the system is set up. Surely if you see a child falling, you catch them before they hit the ground and break several bones. Why? Because if you don't, those bones may never fully repair properly and be permanently damaged. But this is what I had to do with my son. Just watch him struggle and fail and lose himself more and more. I watched him become a shadow of himself, and there was nothing I could do about it.

Every day he would come home with his jumpers chewed to bits, his nails bitten down until they bled and blotches on his skin from the stress. I can't tell you what this does to you as a parent, to watch your child go through this in order to get help that they should be entitled to anyway. This is how Fin was at an excellent school with an SRP, can you imagine how it would have been in a school with no support at all? This is why there are so many school avoiders. The schools are just not equipped for SEND.

The worst thing of all was during this time Poppy was at preschool and her EHCP had been approved. There was no delay, no fighting. One appointment and it was offered. I guess it was quite obvious that an EHCP was needed. During the assessment, I came to the preschool to meet with them. I had been in the same room as Pops for an hour and she still hadn't noticed me there. Her own mother. I had been talking, calling her name but she never responded to me. This was proof for how distant she was, and it would be almost impossible for a teacher to get her attention.

From getting her EHCP, she was offered a SEN school straight away. Once again, no arguments, no appeals. Obviously, I was ecstatic as she needed this and it would be amazing for her, but I couldn't help but feel so guilty towards Fin. I was forced to watch him battle on with no help while Poppy was thriving and given all the support she needed. Both autistic, but very different worlds. One was being helped and supported, the other failed by the system. Why? Because Poppy was more disruptive in class, whereas Fin was well behaved and quiet. How is that fair and how the hell do you explain this to a child?

Immediately the difference between a mainstream and SEN school was like night and day. Poppy would run in happily every morning to greet her teachers. She was in a class of 7 pupils, whereas Fin was in a class of 32. Often Poppy would go in in her wellies or leggings because she refused to wear the uniform and that was fine, no one cared. There was no homework to be forced; if she did it then great, if not then that was OK.

I longed for this for Fin, and luckily his school was amazing and started to let him attend the SRP to help him, even without the government funding. Just this small change helped him so much and just about got him through without becoming a completely broken child until his EHCP was finally approved.

And suddenly school life became a little better. The school mornings weren't filled with trying to pacify my sobbing boy. They were still fucking awful, like every day is before school.

The mornings were still filled with me screaming at them to put their shoes on for the 20th time, realising they needed their PE kit, but I hadn't actually washed it in time so giving it a solid Febreezing five minutes before we leave. The kids fighting in the back of the car the whole journey over who gets to play their music.

Nothing had changed with that, but he wasn't terrified to go in. I also wasn't dreading school pickup, not knowing what kind of meltdown we were in store for that night. Were there still bad days? Of course, everyone has good and bad days regardless, but the shift in his mood was incredible. He was starting to become happier, and even started to make some friends. Friends that he found through attending the SRP, other autistic children that accepted him as he was.

A SEN school had proven to be just right for Poppy too. Her speech improved, and soon she was even reading – something I never expected from my child who was nearly non-verbal until age three. I watched in disbelief as she read out number plates. It had all been in there, we just needed the right way to bring it out.

But I don't want to mislead anyone; Poppy didn't start talking because of the school. If anything, I'd thank CBeebies! There's no magic solution for making a child verbal, and parents shouldn't feel responsible. You can encourage speech, but it's not something you can control.

Even though Poppy was progressing, it was not all plain sailing. I had several unexpected calls to tell me about her behaviour, and this had not got better from pre-school. Poppy really struggled with people in her space or anywhere near her space in fact. She seemed to find it especially hard with children her age or younger. I think they were more unpredictable than older kids and she never knew what to expect from them.

As a result, anytime people got too close and invaded her invisible circle of 'me' space, she would scream the place down. It was a kind of clever way to make sure people left you the hell alone. I wish I had used this tactic in the pubs when I was 18 with all the pervy men trying to chat me up. I should have just made a high-pitched scream that could shatter glass when they got near me, I feel like they would have got the idea quicker than my gentle refusals.

My friends soon got used to this barrier that Poppy had created, even for them as adults. She was happy and friendly to people but if they tried to touch her, she would freak out, which is why I remember a trip with my friend to Bluewater Shopping Centre so vividly.

I remember it clearly as it was the day she actually touched another person, and I was amazed! We went to McDonald's there and took a seat. There was a guy sitting next to us, probably late teens. He was tucking into his food, minding his own business. I think he was reading. We were busy eating when Poppy, completely out of the blue, went over and slapped him. Only a small slap but still a slap. Now, most of you would read this and be horrified, that would be the correct response. 'I'm so sorry, she isn't normally like this.' 'Poppy, we don't hit.' Any of these would be seen as an appropriate response.

I, however, was celebrating the fact she actually touched another person. This was a big deal! I was so busy being proud that she had made contact with another person that I actually forgot to apologise to the poor guy. My friend and I were laughing and cheering, but only thought afterwards what that would have looked like. I imagine he went home and told people that he had met the worst mother on earth who actually cheered when their unruly child went over and slapped him. I mean, who could blame him?

For Poppy, sharing a classroom with other children was always going to be an issue, so it was very fortunate there were only seven in her class. But that was still enough to cause her a lot of upset and violent behaviour. The teachers did their best to deal with this and set up a workstation just for her that she could sit at and wouldn't be near the others. As much as I was pleased they did this for her, I also felt so upset that she needed this. Even in a class of children with additional needs, my child was still the isolated one not behaving like the rest.

I remember the dreaded phone calls from the teacher and would think, 'What has she done now?' One time she was having a full-blown meltdown and broke the toilet door. She also blocked and flooded the toilets from stuffing so much toilet paper down them and straight up bunked off by fleeing the classroom. I thought it was only teens that got up to shit like this at school?!

Next, they will be telling me they caught her round the back graffitiing and smoking a fatty! I laugh about this now, but it really wasn't funny at the time. So many thoughts were running through my head like: 'If she was behaving like this in a SEN school, can you imagine how bad it would have been in mainstream? If she can't cope in a SEN school, what hope is there for her? There are no other options!'

But this is part of a SEN parents' life when your kids start school. Endless worrying about how they're doing in school, constant phone calls, travelling miles to find a suitable school in the first place and then fighting for support at the ones they are in. Worrying is most definitely just part of the norm for a SEN parent.

It's funny how we don't even notice things that seem strange to others. I'm so used to Poppy's loud vocal stims – sometimes like a dinosaur being murdered in a bucket – that I don't even hear them until a friend asks, 'What the hell is that noise?' on a voice note. Then I play it back and realise you can barely hear me over the screeching.

I am talking like the school days are over when, in fact, we are not even halfway through, and Fin is just about to start a whole new chapter in secondary school. And there is nothing more terrifying than secondary school. However, as scared as I am, I know I am also stronger now and that strength keeps growing. With every fight, every judgey person, every person that has neglected my kids has made me that bit stronger. Because we have to be strong, for them and to show them that we don't give up; I want my kids to have this fight within them and always strive for better. I want them to know that they don't have to settle for less, such as putting up with an education that is not correct for them. They deserve better than that; every child deserves the right to an education suited to their needs.

Top Tips

☆ *You don't need a diagnosis to request an EHCP.*

☆ *You can apply for an EHCP through your local authority or GP yourself if the school will not do this.*

☆ *If you are looking for a good mainstream school, try to find ones with an SRP (sometimes this is called a specialist resource base, or SRB) and ask to speak to the SENCo about what they offer.*

☆ *If your EHCP is being appealed, and the LA have asked if you would like mediation, it's worth considering saying no and going straight to Tribunal, as it is likely to avoid any further delays.*

Chapter Four

ODD ONE OUT

One of the biggest things I think you learn when you become a SEN parent is who your real friends and even family are. It can be a very lonely journey, and even lonelier when you lose people you thought you were close to.

I would say the first time it hit me that people start to treat you differently when you have a neurodivergent child was around the first year of school. One of the boys was having a party. His mum was someone I spoke to regularly. We would speak at the gates, message each other and often talk about the boys; even had a couple of play dates with him coming to us and Fin going to them. I then found out about a party they hosted in their garden that Fin had not been invited to. All the other boys had except him. My heart broke. I knew Fin was already struggling to make friends and seeing lots of the kids joining in and bonding together would only push him out further.

I called her and asked why he wasn't invited, and she told me she didn't think he would enjoy it because he's very quiet. I could feel the rage inside. If you are going to exclude a child, then at least have the courage to be honest about why. Do not pretend you did it for my boy. If he wouldn't enjoy it, then he or I will be the ones to make the decision whether he attends or not.

I would love to be able to say to you that I was the bigger person and stepped away from the conversation. I would love to be the sort of person who could chalk it up to experience and move on.

I, however, am not that person. The Mumma bear came out in me, and I believe, through the red mist, I called her at least a bitch before hanging up on her.

I don't regret it.

This is something I noticed more and more. The invites were getting less, and sometimes not even with the fault of the other person. The problem is, when you are raising autistic children, days out are hard and incredibly stressful. Friends would suggest meeting at soft play, and I would be smiling manically and nodding, thinking 'I would rather pull out my own eyeballs and eat them.'

It's only natural that parents of neurotypical children would suggest this though. Soft play is great if you are able to sit at a table and enjoy your coffee. How lovely to catch up with a friend over a cuppa while the kids happily go off and play. What a wonderful, enriching day out for you both.

That is not my experience of soft plays.

Not.

At.

All.

For me there is no sitting. I am forced to chase my kids around a fucking monkey gym, trying to fit my fat arse through the tiny gaps in the netting, while getting pelted in the face with rubber balls made sticky by some unknowable secretions.

The worst thing is when you have two kids because,

of course, they run in different directions. I can hear one screaming across the play centre like he is being murdered, while I am hanging upside down trying to squeeze myself through something that resembles a car wash with Poppy clinging on to my leg.

From my vantage point, hopelessly tangled in some kind of rope netting, being beaten over the head with squishy off-brand versions of cartoon characters, I glance down at my friends below, sitting at the table, laughing with each other. I believe they are on their second cup of tea. Arseholes.

I can see my tea still sitting there, untouched and cold; and I think, well this is fucking great. I haven't even managed to say a word to them, and I might as well have just come here alone. And so might they. It would still be shit but at least I wouldn't get FOMO. (For the oldies reading this, it means fear of missing out. I learned this from my son last week. See, I'm down with the kids.)

So, because of the above, I start saying no to days out like this and suggest other places like a beach day, and then instantly regret this too.

The beach always sounds great. Open spaces to run, minimal opportunities for injury, ice cream on hand.

In reality, it's a shitstorm. A shit sandstorm to be precise. Within five minutes of getting to the beach, Fin will get sand in his eye.

Every.

Single.

Time.

Of course, he will not wear sunglasses so there is not a lot we can do to protect his eyes, but I really don't know how it manages to happen every time, but it does, without fail.

And boy, does he let the world know about it. Going quietly into the night is not for Fin, oh no. We end up pouring our only bottle of water over his eye to get it out. We have to pour the whole thing because he can still feel the tiny grain of sand, even though it's probably left long ago, and so, on a 35-degree day, we end up with no drink. The sand on his face has then got wet, which is another issue, so we need to get the talc out to pour over him to get it off. Seriously, talc is a lifesaver at the beach if you didn't already know. After much screaming and pouring, we have a completely covered in talc, bright white, sobbing child walking to try to find a spot to sit at. Yes, we haven't even made it as far as finding a place to sit yet.

I then have to be the pain-in-the-arse friend that demands we sit right next to the sea because the kids will just go for it and keep running into the sea until they drown, so I need to get to them in time. As we all know, this is always the worst place to sit as the tide starts to come in, so we spend the day having to move all the food, picnic blankets and toys back in 6ft increments to avoid getting washed out to sea.

I mean, the picnic blanket is only really there for my friend anyway as, once again, I can't sit down. I am having to run to each child to get sand out, or off, of them (which is a losing battle, much like trying to tidy up in a hurricane), or stop Poppy from eating a random chip she found on the floor, or wade into the actual sea because Fin decided to ruin the day by lobbing his favourite toy and then crying because it, funnily enough, was going out to fucking sea!

When it is time for lunch, I lay out all the different snacks I have brought for us and carried on this hike to the beach to make sure I had all their safe foods, only for the kids to not touch a thing because there is too much sand everywhere and the snacks are now warm.

Of course, they are still hungry and will moan about it, they just won't, shan't, can't eat that slightly lukewarm strawberry, 'I'm not a fucking animal, Mother.'

Then just when you think the day can't get any worse, they need a wee, and a poo, and a wee again. Both at different times from each other and roughly every 15 minutes. Why? Because the toilets are a 30-minute sodding walk away, and I am sure my kids sometimes just do things to fuck me up.

So, I have learned to not suggest beach days, unless I am feeling very brave. Unfortunately, friends still suggest it . . . so, I end up saying no.

The thing is people always say it will be fine and to not worry. But I do. It is hard work, not only because I am trying to keep my kids happy or just stop them from hurting themselves, but also because I don't want to ruin someone else's day, and this is a lot of pressure.

I can't help but feel rude when I have barely spoken to my friend when I see them. I often feel like the worst company ever because even when I do manage to sit down with them, I am hardly listening to what they are saying. They are talking but I am trying to listen out for my kids the whole time, I am tuned into listening out for screams that only a mother would know or be able to understand.

The difference between a scream of 'help, I have been

mildly inconvenienced' and 'help, I'm being savaged by a pack of wild dogs' is very similar to untutored ears.

I'm also listening for the screams of another child that Poppy has possibly brained with a plastic spade because they got in her way/too close/looked at her wrong.

Out of the corner of my eye, I am checking around for any escape routes where they may run off, or anything Poppy may pick up and eat off the floor, praying there are no cigarette butts laying around.

I am on high alert, code red, defcon 1, at all times. Even though from the outside you simply see me sitting and smiling at you, inside I have all these worries going through my head and trust me, it is not fun. It is exhausting, mentally and physically.

So, I don't actually want to be out. I want to be at home. In our safe space. I know home. I know they can't get out; I know all the hazards. But here, out in the unpredictable, dangerous world – you, my friend, are a distraction. And I can't be distracted when I am trying to be mum.

I instead try to arrange a night out. No kids and time to actually talk with my friends. A few drinks, maybe even a dance. We talk about what to wear as we haven't got dressed up for ages! When shall we book for? We look at our diaries and arrange for the next week. We are both excited, until next week comes. I haven't slept for three days solid and the bags under my eyes have actually turned into rucksacks. I'm in my comfy stained PJs, I don't even know what the stain is. Is it chocolate or poo? Who knows? Or even cares. The thought of getting dressed up makes me feel physically sick. Love Island is on tonight.

I could catch up with it, while eating ice cream, splodged on the sofa. (I'm splodged, not the ice cream.)

I haven't even washed my hair for days. No, I can't go out, not like this. So, I cancel once again. Or better still, my friend is feeling exactly the same and she cancels first. I am sorry but I don't believe there is any better feeling than this, when someone cancels and you didn't want to go anyway. Sadly, it is usually me that is the one that has to cancel though. Some of the time it is because I simply forgot I made the plan in the first place.

Eventually the invites stop. I understand why. There are only so many times someone can say no to you before you stop bothering, but it still hurts.

And so, I feel isolated once again. I love my kids to pieces, and they make me laugh every day, but honestly, their conversation is shit. It is them talking to me about their special interest. Sorry, did I say to me? I meant AT me. They are not looking for a conversation, they are looking for a whiteboard they can empty their thoughts onto, and I am that walking whiteboard. Trust me when I say, they can talk for hours about one single subject.

I try to shut off but occasionally they will ask me a question about it; it is like being back at school again with the teacher wanting to find out how much I was listening to. If I get the answer wrong, they don't just correct me. They repeat the whole thing again, from the beginning. So yeah, the conversation is pretty one sided and I do long at times to have a proper chat that isn't about the King Kong franchise or jellyfish.

I usually turn to Instagram or TikTok at these times to

see what the rest of the world are up to, but social media can be one of the worst places to look when you are feeling alone. I kept scrolling through peoples' pictures of fun days out and kids' parties and realising how many days out we were not invited to.

Feeling left out as an adult is one thing, but I really don't think people understand how awful it feels to see your child being left out, until they experience it. It truly is the most awful feeling, and it's happened to not only Fin, but Poppy too. I am an adult and if you don't invite me, so what. I won't lose sleep over it, but I will remember the kind of person you are. With kids it cuts so much deeper. I think some of it is because we already see all the things they will never be a part of.

Having SEN children, we know it's likely they may never go to gymnastics or be part of a nativity. Their routine may prevent them from attending sleepovers or doing things older kids typically do, like meeting friends at a pub or going on holiday with them. So, seeing them excluded from things they don't actually have to miss out on now feels like another opportunity has been ripped away from them again. It's hard to see it as anything other than cruel and unfair.

Over time, you understand this . . . social exclusion was a blessing in disguise as you see peoples' true colours, and I promise you, you will be glad to know what people are really like. When you hit the hard times, it's important to see who sticks around and who doesn't.

I try to not waste too many thoughts now on those who were so thoughtless with my children. Even family members can be just as much of a disappointment as acquaintances sadly. The people that never call to check how they are, don't remember birthdays, make dismissive if not outright rude snide comments. The kids don't know, but I do. And I get that life is busy. I get that things sometimes get forgotten but still.

People speak about how it takes a village to raise a baby, but when you have an autistic child, you need that village throughout life.

Unfortunately, the village starts to dwindle pretty quickly when the inhabitants realise you need more than minimal support.

I remember my mum telling me that after she gave birth to me, she was in hospital for a whole week with me. Most mums are in and out within a day now. The support just isn't there like it used to be with raising kids.

People are so understanding though of mums that have just had a newborn baby. They appreciate how tired she is, how you need to keep the routine of bottle feeding and sleep. They understand why her house and herself often looks a mess. Because they are so understanding of this, they offer to help. They offer to have the baby while she catches up on some rest. They offer to help clean and even bring meals over, so she doesn't have to cook. The invitations of help are non-stop.

When you have a SEN child, the offers of help stop, but needing the help doesn't. Instead of people appreciating how tired you are, you get told that you are being too soft and just need to get them in a bedtime routine. You are asked why you are not back at work and judged for claiming benefits because you say you can't work. If only people understood that, for many of us, the baby and toddler stage doesn't go. We are still there. We are still wiping bums when they're 10, are still cutting up food at 12, we are still dealing with meltdowns (often mislabelled tantrums) at 15. The only difference is, our children are now almost as big as us, sometimes bigger. They are strong, and these tasks get harder as they get bigger. Especially since many places you go to don't accommodate disabled children. The nappy-changing areas are proof of this. Most places have a changing area big enough for a toddler, but not for a teen or an adult. These disabled people are then forced to lay on a dirty toilet floor, while being changed which is just totally unacceptable. Everything gets harder, but with less support.

The village is a fucking ghost town these days.

But before you give up all hope, please stay. It is not all doom and gloom. I promise there are some incredible people out there. Raising SEN kids shows you the people that are selfish and careless, but it also shows you the people that are angels in disguise.

It's funny how life can bring you together with some people. I feel that there are a lot of people we meet throughout our lives, and they are supposed to be there for one stage we are at, then as our lives move on so do they. But there are the very small number of people that are here for the long run. The ride-or-dies, in it to the bitter end. The Thelma to your Louise.

I met one of my friends at a toddler group, and it was actually her son that forced us together. This little two-year-old kept running over with a huge smile on his face. He was so friendly and wouldn't leave me alone, forcing us to speak to each other. We now believe he is neurodivergent too and I do think that us neurodivergent people are drawn together somehow. My friend was always accepting of Fin and his needs. She never questioned why he was crying so much or why he didn't like to do certain things, and her children treated him like family. I think kids usually do. What you see is what you get with them, they don't care about differences until they get older sadly.

Another friend I met at work and overheard her say that she had a toddler, the same age as Poppy at the time. I don't know why but I asked her, 'Is he OK?' I still don't know what made me ask this, but she replied, 'He's autistic.' And our friendship came from that. I was so happy to find another person who got it. I believe that since having my children, I have become more discerning in my friendships. It has made me find people that are really my people.

Like I said previously, days out can be exhausting, I can't add to that with small talk and worrying about who I'm with. I love the friendships I have because I can simply say, 'I'm done,' and then fuck off back home. No apologies, no upset. They accept that sometimes our trips out will only last 30 minutes, and they accept that they may not hear from me for two weeks after that – and that's OK. Well, it's probably not OK, and I am a bit of a shit friend, to be honest, but they seem to put up with it. Girls, if you're reading this – I'm sorry, and I love you. But I will never get better at replying to text messages. Make your peace with that, as I have.

I think when you are raising autistic children you need to be surrounded by your comfort friends. These are the ones I have that I turn up to, me in floods of tears because we have had a bad morning, or the ones that I can call my kids an arsehole to, and they won't judge me.

I remember the day after I gave birth to Poppy, my friend came over to meet her. I had been waiting nine months to smoke again as I had missed it so much! So, I handed tiny Poppy over to her and asked her to watch her while I sat outside and had my first cigarette. Of course, it made me feel horribly sick and only convinced me to stay away from the things, but she never once judged me for that. She just let me do what I needed to do.

After having Pops, I didn't have anyone that had a baby the same age as her so baby groups would be the only place to meet people, but again it's not easy when your child isn't interacting or behaving like the others. This is why SEN groups are so important. I used to take Fin to baby and toddler groups, and I would often have to leave early because of him getting upset, but when I had Poppy and she started to show autistic traits, we were offered to attend a SEN group called Stepping Stones. I am so pleased we had this, as this is where I could breathe a sigh of relief as everyone was in a similar situation.

Many children were having meltdowns, some chewing things they shouldn't, some trying to run off, none of them paying any attention to the songs we were singing. It was chaos and it was glorious. This was my first experience of attending somewhere that I felt I belonged. It abruptly came to a stop though with lockdown hitting, which was so sad. I do wonder if I would have found more friendships in these groups if we hadn't stopped going.

I had tried, gods know I tried, to keep up with friendships

I had prior to kids, but they just fizzled out like a match in the rain.

These friends were raising neurotypical kids and as much as I think you can still have these friendships, I think my anxiety and depression wouldn't allow it.

I would possibly still have these friends if I was in the headspace I am at now, where I am not struggling so much with their needs. But sometimes, when you are battling with your mental health, you have to let some commitments go in order to cope. It sounds so harsh to say, but they were at the bottom of the list. Obviously, my family is at the top, through to close friendships, work, running a home, school life, doctors' appointments and diagnosis, pets – the list goes on. Something had to give, and the easiest thing to give up is the friendships that cause you anxiety. The ones where I didn't feel like I, or my child, could truly be ourselves.

Skipping on to more recent times, I found a brand-new friendship group and one I never expected. I found a group of friends online. We found each other through social media, all with one thing in common – we all had autistic children. Together we began campaigning for change and created SEND Reform England. We started doing protests across England, we ran petitions and even went to Parliament several times. As I write this, it is still hard to believe that we achieved all this. Through this, a few of us formed a close bond, even though our children are very different. Some are nonverbal, some with high-care needs and some with low-care needs, some boys and girls, some older and younger, yet we all got each other. We understood. We cried together and laughed together. No judgement, just support. It is something I think we did not realise we had needed until it was suddenly here, something that had been missing for all these years of raising our children. People may say online friendships aren't real ones, but this couldn't be further from the truth. I think finding friends online can open you up to finding the most amazing people that you would usually never meet because you are miles apart. I think this will be the way forward for many of our autistic children too, who struggle to make friendships. It's easier to talk to each other behind a screen or in text than in person. There's less pressure.

Being frank, I have always struggled with friendships to some degree. I think this is why I can see so much of myself in my kids sometimes. I can see how Fin puts on a show around friends – like I always did – and I can see how Poppy prefers her alone time often – again, the same as me. It's the constant battle in my head of being lonely but also wanting to be alone. I never thought it was possible to feel both things, but I often do.

Even some family live miles away, and again, you miss the village not being close by. We had to move away from my mum and dad to a cheaper area after we got married. We're only an hour away from them, but it felt like they might as well have been in a different country for the first year of Fin's life. The main problem was that I didn't have a car at the time, and I knew no one in this new area. I would wander the streets with Fin in his pram, trying to keep him calm, just walking for hours but never talking to anyone. I even started to do Avon as I thought I should at least try and make some money while walking around. That turned out to be a bad idea though. Half the time would be me getting caught with little old ladies inviting me in to show me photos of their grandchildren, which is lovely, but when you have a screaming baby, you know you need to keep moving at all times. The rest of the time was having old men shouting at me from their doorstep, telling me they didn't want any junk mail.

My cousin wasn't far, but she worked full time, so I felt lost. The day that I got to see my mum and dad was every Friday and this was one of reasons I started to question if something was going on with Fin. Without fail, we would see my parents every week. They would always be so happy to see him, usually holding lots of presents for him and the cupboards full of all the snacks he loved. But he was still very unsure of them. He wouldn't go running into their arms excited to see them like most kids would with their grandparents; he acted like they were strangers most of the time. And for some reason, I felt guilty. I felt awful that he couldn't give them the kind of love they wanted, and I felt responsible for it. Over time, we started to realise that he was bonding with them but just in his own funny way. Poppy is the same in some ways but even with me as her mum, I will have to force her to say goodbye to me at the school gates and sometimes she will run past me when I go to collect her. I'm like, 'Nice to see you, Pops, cheers for even noticing that I am here!'

The school gates at mainstream I found the hardest, and the parents most cliquey in all honesty. I guess it's always going to happen, and groups will naturally form but being the parent of a child with additional needs, you always feel on the outer edge. It didn't help when I took our new pup, Frankie, there, because he is an arse. He decided to do the biggest, wettest shit right in the middle of the entrance. It was so bad the caretaker had to come out and hose it down.

Seriously!

I saw lots of mums get togethers which I wasn't invited to. I guess I just didn't fit the mould, the same as our kids don't. As time went on, I learned to keep myself to myself at the school drop-offs and honestly, there was some relief in that. Not having to try anymore, and not needing to be liked.

I did, however, join the school WhatsApp groups and as much as they can be overwhelming at times, they were actually a big help to me, who forgets everything. Terry would often hear me shouting 'Shit!' as a message came through reminding us of the school trip booked for tomorrow. I am not proud of the fact that I have forgotten non-uniform day once as well. I felt like the worst parent ever. I tried to convince Fin that it was better to be in uniform, but he wasn't having it. I had to go home, get him some clothes, and come back to do the walk of mum shame.

So, I admit, I can't fully blame the school mums and other people for being the reason my circle got smaller, because some of the reason was me. I am definitely less tolerant than I used to be. I think it's because the kids use up every last bit of patience I have. When you have spent over an hour trying to get your child to put a shoe on, you have nothing left for anyone else.

One thing I will never apologise for though is cutting people out of our lives who are toxic and refuse to educate themselves on autism. As much as it hurts, it is best to not be around people that make you and your child feel uncomfortable.

One friend we no longer see – let's call him Bob – in my opinion, never believed in autism. He seemed to think we were overreacting and feel that 'good discipline' was the answer. When Poppy was born, he would often ask about how she was, showing concern for the normal illnesses and baby issues. But despite Fin's autism diagnosis, something lifelong, I don't remember him asking once how he was doing. It hit me that if it's not visible, people like Bob don't care. We eventually stopped reaching out, tired of making the effort when he never adjusted his loud, aggressive behaviour for our kids. It's funny how people expect our children to adapt, but they won't change a thing.

I think it is easy to get caught up in feeling hurt and let down by friends and family that have not treated your children how you would expect them to; however, eventually, you have to let that shit go – for your own sanity.

They are actually the ones who have lost. They never got to build a relationship with our children, never got to gain their trust and see what incredible kids they are. As you notice the ignorance more in people, your circle will always get smaller; but the one you are left with is far stronger than the one you started with. A steel band, forged in the fire of ignorance and dismissal.

Top Tips

☆ *Always remember, two good supportive friends are better than 20 rubbish ones that aren't there for you.*

☆ *Join the school WhatsApp group as they will be a good reminder for events. Yes, you will have to hear Barbara waxing lyrical about little Tarquin's amazing progress but grit your teeth and do it.*

☆ *Find your tribe – whether it's by joining SEN groups online, in person, whatever. Sometimes you need to search for yourself.*

☆ *If there are no SEN groups in your area, find the courage to start one yourself. I am sure there are many parents who are in the same situation as you. You could simply arrange a coffee morning on a local Facebook page.*

☆ *The biggest one. Learn to say no. Saying no instead of saying yes and cancelling all the time is far better. Be honest with yourself. If you really don't want to go, then don't.*

Chapter Five

UNMASKING THE MASK

I said we would come back to masking, as it needed a chapter all on its own. The reason I said this is because I feel like this is one of the biggest struggles we have had with autism. Masking is basically an autistic person suppressing who they really are. Acting neurotypical, exhibiting learned behaviours to try and fit in.

I think it is born from feeling different to everyone else and wanting to blend in. They will often hide their emotions, or their autistic traits, in front of people but when alone, they can let it all out.

Fin began masking at a young age, around the pre-school time. As with a lot of kids, he would cry every time I left him there, but when I was out of sight, he would stop. The thing is, most kids would actually be OK after they stopped crying and go and play, or get distracted with something else, but Fin wasn't OK - he was just pretending to be. He would go into himself and stay silent. When I would pick him up again, the impossible pressure of his suppressed feelings would finally have an outlet, the dam would burst and he would be unsettled and sobbing the rest of the evening. This only got worse once he hit primary school.

I requested a meeting with Fin's school as I was at a loss of what to do. I felt completely alone and unable to help my child. I knew how desperately unhappy he was there, but he wouldn't tell anyone. He would go in each day, sit at his desk and try to blend into the background. He wasn't making friendships and was struggling with the work. He couldn't even admit that he was finding the work hard. The teacher would speak to the class about their subject, reading through what they needed to do but Fin would be lost. Distracted by everything and unable to focus on what she was saying, he would stare at the piece of paper in front of him with no clue what was expected of him. He was miserable and I couldn't bear to watch my child slowly fade away anymore, so the meeting was had, but I came out feeling worse than when I had gone into it, because I didn't feel they understood.

I even overheard someone saying that it would be impossible to hide your feelings so well all day and then let it out just at home. This shows how little some people know about masking. I was so upset; if only people could see him breakdown and what a struggle it was to get him into school at all.

She even joked that if he was that good at masking, he should get an acting career as he was amazing. I didn't find this funny in the slightest, I just felt utter disappointment that my child was being completely misunderstood. I must admit though, he was good at it. Very good. And this is a skill that you really don't want your child to have. I even began to wish he had more autistic traits. I saw children with high support needs making stimming noises and rocking constantly and I longed for him to show them somehow, like these children did, that he was in distress. I appreciate this sounds mad as a lot of people spend their life trying to suppress some of their children's behaviours, but I knew people wouldn't believe it until they actually saw it for themselves.

I, however, would see it in action. I saw it in action every day. The mornings would be filled with tears, headbutting the walls, saying awful things like he didn't want to be here anymore, but as soon as we drove to school, I would look in my mirror and see him perfecting the mask, wiping the tears away on his sleeve before we arrived to once again fool everyone around him.

It wasn't just at school either, my friend looked after him while I was attending a course one day. When I came to pick him up, he had a huge bruise on his head. She said to me that he had been running and hit his head on her door frame. I wasn't shocked as this was something he did a lot, always walking into something, stubbing his toe, etc. I once watched him bang his head on the ironing board twice within 30 seconds.

She was amazed that he hadn't cried at all. She told me how brave he was and what a high pain threshold he must have. This almost made me fall over backwards, Fin has zero pain threshold. Not even that, minus. Honestly, we have been stopped before because a lady passing by was so worried he had broken something, she asked me if an ambulance needed to be called. As I held my screaming child in my arms, I explained to her that it was fine, he in fact just had a splinter. Sorry, he had previously had a splinter, now he was just having the memory of a splinter and would likely be doing so for some time.

So, I knew he was hiding his feelings again and could see how much that would have hurt him. For him to not cry just told me how uncomfortable he was. It's funny because lots of people think it is a good sign that my child is so well behaved for them. I think the opposite. I know he was too uncomfortable to be his true self with them.

I spent my days before school begging him to let go and show how he was feeling. I tried to explain that no one will help if they don't know he is struggling, I reminded him that he won't be in trouble for crying but he just couldn't let it out. Sadly, it made no difference. I don't think a kid in history has ever listened to their parents.

I think this can sometimes be the problem with low-care-needs children. They feel the need to fit in with everyone else, they don't want to stand out in any way or be noticed. It comes with being seen to be 'normal' enough to go to mainstream school, but not 'normal' enough to feel it. It's almost as if they know they are playing a part, trying to fool everyone into thinking they belong there when they don't. The performance is exhausting, draining their spirit and undermining their strength.

Whereas, when I look at Poppy, she couldn't give a shit what anyone thought. If she didn't like something, the whole world would know. If she fancied dancing with her shoes on her hands in the playground, then she would. That's why I can't agree with people calling autism mild for the children with low-care needs. From the outside, Poppy would be classed as more severe than Fin. She had speech delay and some learning difficulties, appearing to day-dream a lot and not be 'with it' whatever 'it' is, whereas Fin had reached all his milestones and was academically fine.

But if you asked me who suffered with their autism more, it would be Fin.

Fin's anxiety would keep him up at night and he would carry the weight of the world on his shoulders. He still does. He fixates over problems that haven't even occurred yet and is terrified of breaking the rules or changing the routine. He notices others and knows that he is different, so the masking is all part of trying to hide who he really is.

I tell my kids every day that they should be proud of who they are and embrace their differences, but it doesn't sink in. Terry and I even try to show them how we don't care what people think of us; we thought that may be enough to show them that it really doesn't matter if you make a fool of yourself sometimes, but I think we just ended up embarrassing him more.

After school one day, he told me that he doesn't feel like the rest of the children, and this is when I decided to talk to him about his autism.

I said this to him: 'Some people have different brains. Some people are neurotypical, and some people are autistic, and you are one of the autistic people. This is brilliant in some ways as it means, for example, you have better hearing than others. You can hear sounds that I sometimes can't. This will be amazing for you when crossing the road to listen for cars or hearing amazing sounds like rain falling. But it may also cause you some problems. A classroom filled with lots of children will sound much louder to you than the others and you will find it harder to concentrate because of that noise, so you may need to wear ear defenders at times. This doesn't mean that you are worse than anyone else, it just means that you need some small adjustments to make learning fair for everyone. This is also the reason you sometimes don't enjoy parties like the other children do. You are having to deal with a lot more than others because it is not just your hearing that is better, but all of your senses are.'

I tried to explain it this way to put a spin on some of the negatives that come with being autistic. I'm always a little reluctant to call it their superpower, even though I know some people do. My kids are literal thinkers, and I know they'd be expecting to do something pretty spectacular with their powers – and would be quite disappointed if I told them their power was not being very sociable or liking routine. I mean, I agree – out of all the superpowers, like being able to fly or being invisible, being told you spin a lot is pretty shit, really. It's no laser eyes.

I went on to explain, 'There are some incredible, intelligent autistic people out there that have achieved amazing things, and you will too as long as you get the right support for you.'

And do you know what he said to me after this long speech?

'OK.'

That was it. There was me working myself up, jotting down ideas of how to break this life-changing news to him, worried if I should even tell him at all. Would it make him feel less than other people? Would he feel ashamed of himself, and could it go on to cause mental health problems later down the line? But that was all he had to say.

OK.

No questions, no emotions. He just walked off after.

I laugh about it as it is typical of him to be very matter-of-fact about it, and I shouldn't have spent so long worrying.

I do, however, believe telling him really helped him understand himself more. He seemed almost more relaxed with himself and hopefully understood that he wasn't struggling because he was stupid. And very slowly the mask started to slip.

I explained to him about the importance of others knowing that he is struggling. I told him a story about five children running a race and he was one of them. All the children had the same backpack on but there was one difference – Fin's backpack was full of rocks. At the beginning of the race, all the children were running equally as fast but the longer the race continued, the heavier those rocks felt to Fin, so he started falling behind. At the end of the race, Fin came last. He felt ashamed and disappointed in himself for being the slowest. He couldn't understand why all the other children raced through fine, but he was really struggling. The teacher asked what he was struggling with, and he replied that the bag felt heavy, so the teacher looked in the bag and couldn't believe her eyes. She lifted it and was shocked how heavy it was, and she then checked everyone else's bag and found them empty. The teacher explained to Fin that because she knows what caused him to struggle now, she can fix it for next time. Next time she will make sure his bag is empty, and he may still come last but even if he did, at least he wouldn't have struggled the whole way to get to the end.

I was told by the Head Teacher that usually the mask starts to drop around year 2. I didn't quite believe her at the time in all honesty. I couldn't understand how a child who had perfected fitting in could suddenly lose that in year 2, but it really did happen with Fin. I wonder if it's maybe as the work gets harder, or possibly just part of growing up and hormones, but the weight of the mask becomes too much to hold up all day. He started crying a lot more at school and I was overjoyed. This may sound like the strangest thing ever, but to me, it meant two things . . .

1 He was feeling more comfortable there, enough that he could now show more emotion.

2 He might start getting more support.

The teachers were noticing other things too. The constant chewing on his clothes (his really expensive uniform clothes I would like to add!). His rocking back and forth when anxious and his constant need to move and fidget while seated.

They gave him some playdough to fiddle with, but it wasn't enough. I would also see this for myself when coming to school plays. I have a video of all the children singing in the nativity, standing straight and looking forward. Except one child at the back – my boy. Swaying back and forth repeatedly. To the untrained eye, he probably looked like he was having a great time and rocking away to 'Silent Night', but I knew this wasn't a happy boy. This was a very uncomfortable child not coping and stimming madly to regulate himself.

This is why people still need to learn about masking. A lot of people think that masking is coping but it isn't. It is simply suffering in silence, and it is not healthy at all. It is the same as keeping all your emotions in and never letting anyone know how you really feel. Pretending to be OK when you are anything but.

A lot of people use the coke bottle effect as an analogy. Throughout the day, the different tasks are causing the coke bottle to shake. Every single thing, from talking to other classmates, having to sit at a desk, to wearing an uncomfortable uniform is making that coke bottle shake more and more. When you get home, you open that coke bottle, and it explodes everywhere. This is what happens when our children get home, they can open up and release all their emotions from the day.

The biggest issue with masking is it will always delay diagnosis. I was so terrified going to the latest assessment. I was sure he would put an act on. I imagined that he would do something mad like go straight over to the paediatrician, shake his hand and say, 'Lovely to meet you, Sir.' Luckily, these are professionals and most of the time they can see through it, which they did with Fin.

I talk more about Fin when it comes to masking, as Poppy has never really tried to hide who she is. However, the older she gets, the more I am concerned she is starting to, but in very different ways to Fin. For example, we went to meet my family at Eastbourne. My aunties were there who we don't see very often, so for Poppy, they were practically strangers. We went to meet them at a cafe on the seafront, and instantly when meeting them, she dropped her trousers and pants and showed them her bum. Obviously, everyone was laughing, including me, but I did start to wonder is this a show? Does she do this as she knows it will make people laugh? Maybe she isn't as confident as I initially thought.

I can see this in myself to be fair. I often play the part of the joker. If I laugh at myself, then no one will be laughing at me, they will be laughing with me. I guess it's a self-protection thing when you lack confidence in yourself. As I am writing this, I'm realising how cringe this is sounding, like I'm the main character in an indie film. Oh God, stop me now please, before I start singing with my eyes closed.

The thing is, I understand the masking. I do it every day without even realising. There are many social events that I go to and wish I wasn't there. I hate small talk and meeting new people. Do I let anyone know? Of course not. I smile and pretend I am happy to be there. In fact, I have masked so well throughout my life that people actually label me as confident. This couldn't be further from the truth. I have terrible anxiety going to new places and meeting new people. If one of my friends tells me they have invited another of their friends along to our meet up, I instantly don't want to go. It fills me with dread. Even to the point that my friend and I had an argument because we had arranged a day out in London with the kids.

You can imagine how stressful that is anyway, taking the kids on a train to London, but she then told me she had invited her friend with her kids to come too. I was absolutely appalled. The audacity. The insolence. The sheer unmitigated gall.

I hated going into London with the kids, the only reason we went there is because the museums are so great and interactive, but I am always terrified the whole time we are there. Trying to cling on to the kids' hands because of so many people and fretting that the transport would be delayed was enough stress already, without me now having to actually make conversation with a stranger.

Hell no. So, I did an awful thing and told my friend that she needed to uninvite her friend. I was so freaked out by this that I completely forgot about the position this would be putting my poor friend in. How awful is that? I laugh with her about this now, but at the time we had a huge row and didn't speak to each other for months, all because I didn't want to talk to a stranger for the day! And I wonder where my kids get it from.

Or not, I guess. It's pretty obvious.

This has often worried me that I have somehow made them mask who they are without even knowing I am doing it. Things like hiding in the house when the doorbell rings because I don't know who it is. Fin once answered it, and it was our neighbour. Fin told her I had been hiding from her. 'Erm, no. Of course I wasn't, Fin. I thought it was a Jehovah witness!' I say through clenched teeth. After she leaves, I'm like, 'Oh my god, why did you answer the door?' I mean, how confusing is this to a kid, especially an autistic kid? I wondered if by him seeing me mask like this, it made him mask too. I really hope not.

So, it has taken me 40 years, but I am now learning to drop the mask. If for nothing else but to show my kids that we are perfectly fine being us and we don't have to pretend to be anyone else. And we certainly don't need to pretend to be normal . . . whatever that is anyway. As the quote says from *Alice in Wonderland*: 'You're entirely bonkers, but I'll tell you a secret – all the best people are.'

Top Tips

☆ *If your child is a masker, record moments at home of stimming or meltdowns to take with you to the autism/ADHD assessment.*

☆ *It sounds obvious but remind your child every day that they don't have to pretend, and they will not be in trouble for showing their emotions. Some children are terrified of getting into trouble. We need to remind them that being overwhelmed or upset is not bad behaviour.*

☆ *Give them a notebook that they can write down their thoughts and feelings in if they find it hard to communicate it.*

☆ *Find a safe person (key worker) that your child can go to at school if they feel anxious.*

Chapter Six

TANTRUMS OR MELTDOWNS?

Now I know my children are not saints, trust me. Sometimes they are arseholes. I think all kids can be at some point in their life, autistic or not. There is a big difference between things they can and cannot help, but finding out what is because of the autism and what is just being a kid can prove to be very tricky at times. Especially when they are young.

People often ask me on social media what the difference is between a tantrum and a meltdown. I usually find a tantrum will go away after you give them what they want, whereas a meltdown won't. In fact, a meltdown can seem like it's about this one thing, so you give in or do that thing you think they want, expecting it to calm your child, but it wasn't about that at all.

Sounds confusing, doesn't it? It bloody is.

I think the toddler stage is probably the hardest to judge. As toddlers do have a lot of meltdowns anyway. They are still learning how to cope with their emotions and understanding what they do and don't like. Toddlers also usually do not have good communication; some may not speak at all. Mix this with autism, and you are in for a fun ride (said no SEN mum ever). This is one of the reasons getting a diagnosis in early childhood is quite difficult, as a lot of the typical toddler behaviours are very similar to autistic behaviours.

Someone once said to me that it feels like their autistic child never left the toddler years and I totally get that. Toddlers have a lot of sensory seeking habits, much like many of our autistic children. Their communication and the way they play is very much like many children with ASD, playing alongside other children instead of with them, for example. Not to mention the fact that toddlers are very bouncy and fidgety. If you see them in a café, you can see they want to get down from the high chair and run around and the parents are usually trying to distract them with books or toys, much like we have to when taking our children out. The difference is people will smile at toddlers and tell the parent how funny and adorable they are. No one smiles at an autistic 15-year-old, jumping up and down, stimming in a café. You will still get the looks, but they won't be the kind you want.

There will be looks of horror and judgement, fear even. This is not bad behaviour though, the same as it isn't for a toddler, but when they are older it is treated like it is. Like they should magically know better.

So, then we move on to what is bad behaviour? And there are many grey areas, which makes it so hard. Bad behaviour is hitting someone at the age of ten. We know this is not acceptable. OK, but what if that child has a developmental age of an 18-month-old baby? How do you discipline? It needs to be the same as an 18-month-old as the understanding is not there. However, what about the SEN-betweeners. They are verbal, they understand when you say no. They go to mainstream school. They, however, haven't learned to control their temper yet. When they are overwhelmed, they lash out as they go into fight or flight mode. How do you discipline this? We have to teach them right from wrong, but we also have to be understanding to their needs.

In this particular instance, I would wait for them to calm down before speaking to them. Doing this while they are in fight mode would be pointless as they are not listening. I would remove them from the situation. I would then explain to them that I understand they were angry, but this behaviour was unacceptable, and they must apologise. Do I give them a punishment and take away something they love, for example? In my opinion, no. Not unless they keep repeating this behaviour, but I need to give them longer than a typical child to learn these lessons.

People make allowances for toddlers hitting or biting, but they don't with older children, and it's a shame that they don't appreciate a lot of our children are still mentally at that stage. It's even harder when you are raising giants like I am. Fin is 11 and in age-14 clothes. People expect a lot more from them and don't find their stims as 'cute' as they once did when they were small.

Unfortunately, as with most parenting things, we have had to learn the hard way by making a lot of mistakes. Mistakes that have resulted in hours of meltdowns sadly. I would say Fin was the guinea pig mostly with this, as by the time Poppy was here, we were in tune with the 'tisms a lot more. Fin, if you are reading this when you are older, I am so sorry, but please remember that you were always the one who made me into a better mum. Also remember,

I filled out your baby book, which I never did with Poppy. The poor second child! Sorry, Pops!

I would often find what would be classed as 'naughty' behaviour would usually come out when we were out in busy places. Of course, that makes sense now that it was probably sensory overload causing it, but at the time we didn't know.

The shopping centres were awful with him. Every time I would step into a shop, he would scream the place down. Instead of leaving though, I would try to push through. All I heard from the older generation was 'don't give in and spoil him', 'they have to get used to these things', 'back in my day, they would have had a good slap'.

Honestly, you could see my eyes roll from space when I heard that old chestnut.

Thankfully, I didn't listen to the last bit of advice. Nevertheless, I was scared of giving in too much. I kept thinking that if I gave in, he would never learn to adapt, we would never be able to take him anywhere, but I now wish I had given myself a break. I didn't need to chuck him in the deep end; he needed to adjust slowly and me too.

I wasn't in the right state of mind to be throwing us both into the fire and then trying to rescue us out of it again. It's like when the air steward on a flight tells you to fix your own oxygen mask first before your child's. You cannot save your child if you have already passed out, and I was very much on my way to passing out. I didn't need to make life harder for us, it was hard enough already. I wish I had stayed home with him more, taken time to understand him, what he liked and what he didn't. I shouldn't have kept forcing him into these situations.

Interestingly enough I was having a conversation with my friend about this the other day, and she said that some shops use a high-pitched noise to keep birds away that autistic children may hear but we can't. I have no idea if this is true or not, but it would make a lot of sense and confirm that it wasn't something he could control.

I feel like I spent most of his early years tired and stressed out. The tiredness was coming from getting barely any sleep, which again I thought was just possibly him being a toddler. We had tried everything. Bedtime routines, a calming bath, no screen time, putting his bedtime forward and then putting it back but nothing would work with this kid. So, what other reason could there be that my child just refused to sleep?

Oh yes, he's an arsehole.

So, one night, I lost it. I really shouted at him, screamed even. I still remember his scared little face which haunts me to this day. I scared him, but more than that, I scared myself. Seeing him like that upset me to my core, so I grabbed him and cuddled him to let him know it was OK. I don't like to blame the tiredness for my actions, but it really doesn't help when you are exhausted and it's the middle of the night.

The problem is sometimes other people see their behaviour as bad, when we know it's actually something they are unable to control.

The stimming can be a tricky one, though. They need to do it to regulate, but we also do have to respect other people in the space too.

For example, if Poppy decides to do her loud, screaming stims that sound like a cat trying to poo through a sewn-up bum, when we need to try to keep her quiet in a library or restaurant as people expect a certain experience there, and it's unfair for us to let her run the place.

We have to remember that, even though she really can't help it, others have paid for their meal and deserve to enjoy it without disruption. So, we do our best to try and manage the situation by distracting her, reminding her to be quieter or taking her outside for a bit to get some of the stims out. But if we are walking around Tesco, is there any point in making her upset and trying to stop her? I don't believe so. Yes, it may be annoying for people for the 20 minutes they are mooching about, but they don't have to live with it. So really, they should consider themselves lucky. Don't fucking look at me like that Janet, once you've paid for your sourdough, you'll never have to hear this noise again, but this is my life.

I have actually invested in headphones for me, and they are probably the best purchase I have ever made. If I win the lottery, I will happily pay for them for everyone else if we do decide to ever go to a fancy restaurant with the kids.

Even a so-called friend once used to tell Fin off for being too loud. I find this a massive insult as it's implying that I am just a rubbish parent that doesn't tell my child off. That he's doing it due to a lack of discipline.

I do in fact tell my children off, but I do it when they do something wrong, and stimming is not doing something wrong. He was the kind of person that still believed kids should be seen and not heard though, not my type of guy at all. I actually love to hear kids, I love hearing them laughing and squealing with happiness, I just don't like the whining. It's safe to say, we don't see that friend anymore.

I find it too much hard work around people like that. I would find myself snapping at Fin and being really strict when we were around them and I didn't like the kind of mum I was with that friend there.

I do think some people assume a lot of SEN parents are too soft with their kids and don't give them enough discipline. The thing is these people don't realise we have just mastered picking our battles. When they see our child walking around the shops with no shoes on, they don't see the hours prior to this to even getting them out of the house.

The fights to brush their teeth, get dressed, have breakfast, do their hair. Each instruction causing meltdowns. By the time they have left the house, mum is exhausted. She just needs to get milk, that is all. She hasn't been able to get anything else done all morning because of comforting and negotiating with her child who is still sobbing.

Her child now doesn't want to wear shoes. She managed to get her socks on, but it took 40 minutes. Half the day is gone but she still needs the milk. So, finally, mum gives in. Sod the shoes. We need some milk.

But the public just see the child with no shoes and a weak parent that lets their child get away with everything.

And yes, I am weak at times because I want an easy life. Who doesn't? So, I will absolutely give in to them having crisps at 8am on the odd occasion. OK, every weekend. All right, it's every day, get the hell off my back about it. Don't judge me! I know it's early but in fairness, they usually get up around 5am so it's practically lunch time for them anyway. The thing is, in the grand scheme of things, does it matter that much? Especially with Poppy and her problems with eating – I am just happy she is eating.

This is pretty much my feelings when we are out too, and they are happy. My rule is: Does it hurt them or someone else? No, then it's probably OK. It's a controversial subject for some reason but we always take tablet computers out with us to eat. Every single time. It means the kids are more likely to sit nicely and eat their food and I can actually eat my food while it is hot. As long as it is not too loud for others, I don't see the difference between that or taking colouring books. But some people love to be smug about it when their children don't need to have a tablet or iPad to eat. I find it such a weird flex. 'My child can sit nicely colouring in a picture of a donkey, they don't need a screen in front of them!'

Clap.

Clap.

Clap.

Well. Done. You! If only all parents could have a bright child like yours that can use crayons. I usually respond by saying that my children are actually watching something very educational. They requested the life and works of Beethoven, don't you know? When in actual fact they are watching some really freaky heads coming out of toilets and attacking people on YouTube. (If you didn't understand the reference then that would seem very odd, but it is something called Skibidi toilet. I would recommend never watching this. It is something that once you have seen, you can't unsee.) And who bloody cares if they are watching crap on it? I watch crap every day on the TV, but no one is judging me. Actually, I think Terry judges me quite a lot.

Another thing that people often don't talk about with

raising verbal autistic children is how rude they can come across. I have honestly wanted the ground to swallow me many times because of the kids having absolutely no filter. There is a difference once again between the two. Someone that is rude will tell you what they think even though they are fully aware that this may upset the other person, whereas my children don't have any concept of this. They say what they see or say what they think and would be completely oblivious to how they may make someone else feel.

Once we were in the changing rooms, the kids had just had their swimming lessons and Poppy was fascinated by a lady sitting down drying herself. This lady was very large, so I was already concerned with the fact that Poppy was staring so much. Poppy went over to her and sat behind her. I knew she was going to do something, but it happened almost in slow motion like a film in which there was no stopping her. She grabbed this poor lady's overhanging back fat and shouted 'boobies' at the top of her voice while, I would like to add, still clinging on to the lady's extra skin. Relief washed over me as the lady turned to Poppy laughing. I explained she is autistic and apologised, but after I wondered if that even made sense. I am sorry my kid just assaulted you by grabbing your body and shouting boobies to everyone. Autistic people do that, don't you know? I mean, how weird if you don't know anything about autism – oh, I had no clue they run around grabbing people shouting boobies, I should have maybe explained that she doesn't have any boundaries or social awareness.

I can't even tell you the number of times that Poppy decides to just randomly shout out everything that is slightly different, or has captured her interest, because it really does happen every day at some point. It's like she is playing a game of catchphrase that no one even knew we were playing and just says what she sees. No one is safe . . . bald people, different skin colours, short people, disabled people, bad smells, old people, the list goes on and my face gets redder.

This isn't just Poppy either, Fin has also done this. We went to a family member's house once and they weren't the tidiest of people. As we walked in, he exclaimed very loudly how dirty it was. I believe he said that it was even dirtier than our house. Cheers, Fin. Now that he is older, he understands that he can't actually say these things to people's faces. The issue is, he does something that is far worse. He whispers right in front of them to me, but it's not an actual whisper. It is more of a stage whisper that they can most definitely hear. I don't know why it is worse, but it feels worse. The pointing definitely doesn't help either. He will also do this when he wants to leave some-where or doesn't like their food. I try to explain to him that they are sitting right next to us, but he just doesn't seem to get it.

These things take time for them to understand. Seeing from someone else's point of view instinctually, in the moment, and using that insight to navigate the social envir-onment is something neurotypical people take for granted.

Even a concept as simple as hide-and-seek took a very long time for them to grasp, and even now their grip is tenuous at best. Anytime one of them went to hide, we would walk into the room and they would instantly shout 'I'm behind the curtain' or in Poppy's case, you would just follow the giggles, unless of course she had completely forgotten what she was doing and abandoned the game all together, or had crouched in plain sight but shut her eyes. Can't see you, can't see me. Fool proof.

I also have to be so careful with what I say around them, as they will happily repeat it to the person I am talking about. 'Mum said you really pissed her off the other day!' Oh great, I really didn't want to have this conversation, but it looks like we are having it anyway.

In all seriousness, it can cause problems and not all people are going to be as friendly and open to their very direct bluntness. Some people take offense, and I can understand why. I take offense and they are my kids. Every day I wake up to Poppy telling me how old I look without make-up and how big my bum is, it starts to give you a complex after a while. But as much as we can try to teach them about how this can hurt people's feelings, it is not something they will learn overnight, and it is still something they cannot help.

I am not going to lie; it is tiring having to work doubly hard to teach our children things that come quite naturally to others. I even taught Fin to hug me, something you would never imagine anyone needing to learn but he really did. He didn't like to be cuddled when he was a baby, as I said before, and over time, he struggled with how to be comforted. Every day we worked on touch and built up to cuddles slowly.

Because of our children's needs, I feel like the way we teach has to be extra because it is extra tough for them to learn. Everything's repeated over and over, and we always need to be one step ahead. There are certain things that you have to be so rigid with, otherwise it becomes a routine before you even realise what was happening. This would happen when I was putting them to bed. I started off saying goodnight and adding to it 'sweet dreams of ice creams', then Fin wanted to add to it 'bouncy balls' and the night after each one of his teddies. Every night he was adding other things to say goodnight to, until I suddenly realised I was spending 20 minutes just saying goodnight. So, we had to go back to the beginning and just say 'sweet dreams of ice creams' again, but this then caused him to think he couldn't go to sleep without saying all the rest. Honestly, people have no idea that the smallest change can disrupt everything. Sometimes you just have to do it and endure the meltdowns that come from it, in order to break through and out the other side into, well, a new routine or process or structure, but one less difficult to manage than the current one.

I will say though, I have noticed that some parents of SEN children are afraid of their children. Now, I am not talking about when children are violent – that is something very different and something you would definitely need support for.

I am talking about parents too afraid to say no to their child, and I get it. You know that it is going to lead to a meltdown and that is scary. But trust me when I say, you have to say no at times, and it will be harder if you always give in. One day you won't be able to, and then all hell breaks loose. I remember the tiptoeing around Fin in the beginning and I spoke about it in the first chapter, so I am not judging anyone. I know how hard it is when you are trying not to trigger them. It will happen anyway though, whether it happens now or in a few hours. Eventually they will have to come out of the bath, or they will have to leave the park, and learning to be firm can be a game changer for you both. Your child won't die from screaming or having a meltdown, but it will be a harder life for them if they are always expecting to get what they want, and I promise this comes from a place of caring – not judgement.

I have been there with Fin and Poppy, and my god Poppy is scary when she is in a mood. But I soon realised I was doing them an injustice by thinking that they would never cope with being told 'no' and by being the soft mum. There are rules at school and in the world that have to be adhered to, and it was my duty to try to prepare them for this uncaring world as best as I could.

This is a neurotypical world, and a tough place to be as a neurodivergent person. We still need to parent and teach right from wrong, but at the same time cut them a bit of slack. The rest of the world certainly doesn't, so we, as their caregivers, can at least do that for them and pick our battles, making life a bit easier for us, while still preparing them for life in neurotypicville.

Top Tips

☆ *Pick your battles. Does it hurt them or anyone else? If the answer is no, then maybe let somethings go.*

☆ *Understand that not everything is because they are autistic – all children will act up sometimes. Don't be afraid to tell them off.*

☆ *If they are doing unwanted behaviours, try distraction techniques and react in an extreme way to show you disapprove of this.*

☆ *Use social stories to help your child understand where you are going and what you expect from them. You can find these online – they are usually picture-based stories that help a child understand what their day is going to be like. For example, if you are visiting a library, you could show pictures of a library and a picture of someone shushing to show it is supposed to be quiet there.*

Chapter Seven

LIFE IS TOO SHORT TO
BE NORMAL

I never knew how confusing autistic children could be until I had them. They are literally walking contradictions a lot of the time, but we, as the parents, are somehow expected to know what they are thinking, what they would like us to do, and if we get it wrong, bloody hell! Our life is not worth living.

Take, for example, them hating noise. Mine have never liked hand dryers, music too loud or busy environments with lots of people, as the noise is too much for them, so, they often wear their ear defenders. However, they are without a shadow of a doubt the loudest people I have ever met. They are right next to me but shouting like I am a few miles away. They have YouTube on full volume and complain they still can't hear it. Yet, I leave a tap running upstairs with the door shut and they will become distressed with the sound and ask me to switch it off.

This often leads to people not quite believing us when we say they are sensitive to noise. We often use the disabled toilet for Poppy because we know the hand dryer won't go off suddenly and upset her. If you have ever used the disabled toilet for your children, you will probably at some points have been faced with the disgusting looks from the elderly as to why we are using it. Sometimes I have even had to explain myself and say that Poppy can't cope with the noise. While I am explaining this though, Poppy is marching out of it screaming at the top of her lungs making me look like a liar.

Another contradiction is their body temperature, and this is mainly Fin. It is like he is running at a completely different temperature to the world; I've considered that he may in fact be some kind of reptile. In the middle of winter, the coldest of days and snowing outside, he will be walking around with a little T-shirt on and at night he will put his four fans on (I'm not exaggerating by the way; he really does have four fans), and the windows wide open. I'm surprised they don't wake up in the morning with bloody frostbite. As they share a room, I feel sorry for poor Poppy who is tucked up in her 20 blankets to stop her from getting hypothermia.

I wouldn't mind but it makes me look like an absolute dick of a mum walking around with him. It's literally minus 2 degrees, ice on the ground. I'm all wrapped up in my winter coat, scarf, hat and gloves, and then Fin is walking next to me in his beachwear. I end up carrying his coat with me and shouting 'put your coat on' really loudly as we walk past people in case someone reports me for neglect.

Of course, in the summer, it's the complete opposite again. A heatwave has hit England and Fin is sitting inside in his cave, refusing to come out into the paddling pool I spent three hours filling up, wearing a hoodie! I beg him to come and try it after he had asked me to bloody put it up in the first place, so he reluctantly dips a toe in and tells me it is too cold!

These contradictions started from a young age as well. Poppy refused to drink her milk, hated most food unless it was a chicken nugget, but would happily eat a bit of bird poo off the floor. Oh yes, she did this once and I can't tell you how frustrated I was! She won't even eat chips, not even McDonald's ones but would eat bird poo! Honestly, I wonder at times if the kids are just trying to screw with us. Just when you think you have overcome something or found something they like, they change their mind again.

Before I knew much about autism, I thought they had special interests that lasted forever, like train spotting for example. I didn't realise their obsessions can change a lot, or even monthly in some cases . . . it's so hard to keep up with. Sometimes I actually start really enjoying a series that he has become fixated with. We learn all the characters, start researching everything about it and I really start to enjoy it myself. Just as we are getting ready to watch the next episode, he has suddenly moved on and that's it, it is done, and never to be watched again. I am gutted so I end up watching the rest alone. Yes, I feel a bit silly watching a children's show by myself, but I bloody do anyway and don't judge me for it! Why should the kids get all the enjoyment anyway?

It's always a nightmare at Christmas and birthdays, as we have to leave it to the very last minute to get him presents related to his special interest. I would love to buy them in bits throughout the year and build it up, so we don't have to suddenly find all the money in one go but it's just not possible. We made this mistake one year, I thought I was safe to get everything that was Plants vs. Zombies; it had been a special interest that had lasted quite a while, and you can't just pick up these toys from Smyths or Argos. It's an old game, so you have to get them from China because, of course, my child would choose something that is really difficult to get hold of. Therefore, we had to order it in early, I think it was about three or four months prior to Christmas and just as December approached, he stopped playing it and moved on to Minecraft. I tried everything to get him back into it again – even the naughty elves did some Plants vs. Zombies drawings around the house but nope, he was done with it. So, we had lots of the Plants vs. Zombies toys that no one wanted to play with, less money and needed to buy lots of Minecraft shit. Brilliant.

Having said that, occasionally he does revisit the obsessions, which I am very pleased about, as otherwise it would be a complete waste of money. It does mean though, that we have about 100 storage boxes full of toys in our tiny two-bed house. We can't even get into the loft anymore because of all the boxes in there, but once he starts to go back to something he previously liked, we have to wade through all the old boxes to find the toys again. I say 'we'; I mean Terry. There is no way I am going up there with all the spiders!

Poppy's special interest has remained the same for many months now. If you follow me on social media, you will know instantly what I'm referring to. SpongeBob SquarePants. We have lived and breathed him for some time now. I think I could recite every episode off by heart. I honestly think I get a bit of Stockholm syndrome with my kids though, because I actually love him too. Not enough to want to watch it on repeat every day but I do love all the SpongeBob merch I have to say. This is where a special interest becomes more that just enjoying something, our kids end up living and breathing it.

The teachers have also had to adapt all their teaching to work around SpongeBob to try to get her engaged. For instance, instead of simply counting, she will need to count how many Patricks there are. In some cases, though, she just decides to incorporate SpongeBob into it herself. I recently had a lot of her schoolwork sent home to find that her answer to the question of how to spell chips was simply a drawing of SpongeBob eating some chips.

Her love for SpongeBob creeps into other interests too, like sea creatures and even sea sponges. We now have a collection of them on her bed shelf, which does look quite odd. Who sleeps here? Someone who has a huge passion for exfoliating.

Our home is filled with so many random things that I barely notice anymore, as it just becomes the norm, but I can imagine as a new person entering it must be very confusing as to who we are as people. For the oldies that will get my reference, it's a bit like a round of 'Through the keyhole,' who lives in a house like this? Come on, I will take you through it. It will be fun.

Enter into our lounge and in front of you are two giant balls. Yes, you heard that right.

Big. Fat. Balls.

Yoga balls. And we have to have two of them. One each, as otherwise the kids will spend the whole time fighting over them. In an already cramped house, you can imagine how much of a pain in the arse these are but on the flip side, they have also been a god send. The kids use them to regulate by summing and they have actually helped to control some meltdowns. Feeling totes emosh? Bounce it out.

Then also in the lounge we have the spinning chair; I believe this is its technical name. It is basically a round stool that spins and again, takes up quite a bit of room. Fin loves this and will spin ridiculously fast on it – I honestly don't know how he doesn't come off it. But again, it leads me to another contradiction.

Fin is the clumsiest person you would meet; he literally trips over his feet every day. He bumps into furniture that we have had in the same place in our house for the last ten years, like he has never seen it before. The days are filled with him stubbing his toes, bumping his head, falling over and twisting his ankle. I am still considering getting him referred for dyspraxia but, in all honesty, I just don't know if I have it in me to go through another battle and paperwork. Another reason I haven't got him referred is because of the contradiction again, he can go 100mph spinning on his chair and be doing it for a good 10–15 minutes, yet will get up from it and walk in a straight line. How? I have no idea, but he doesn't even get dizzy!

Anyway, getting back to our very small lounge filled with sensory equipment. We also have stepping stones; these are very large steps that run across the floor. The kids love to hop from one to the other. We also have five toy boxes in the lounge full of chew toys, fidget spinners, dinosaurs, light up balls, slime, playdough and random twigs and stones that Poppy has found from outside. She is like a squirrel hoarding its nuts. She finds it, brings it in and hides it away. She doesn't touch it again, but we are also not allowed to get rid of it. And on top of all the sensory equipment we have, we also have about 20 chargers, tablets, switches, Xbox and computer, so, most of the time I really feel like the old lady in *A Squash and a Squeeze*. I actually think I am starting to look more like her recently too.

It is only as I am writing this down that I have realised how much we actually do have in our lounge, you get so used to seeing it all every day that you stop noticing it. I am now thinking about visitors coming over and having to swim through it all to find our sofa. Who am I kidding though? We don't really have visitors as there is nowhere for anyone to sit.

Even though the toys are here for the foreseeable, the quirks come in stages. Poppy has been through many stages with her footwear and spent a few months only wearing wellie boots at one stage, even during the summer. Shoes have always been a huge battle though for both kids; I think we could have possibly bought a bigger house if it weren't for all the shoes we have had to buy over the years. The issue is, new shoes always feel weird, and you have to wear them in order for them to not feel weird, but our kids with sensory issues can't wear them because they feel weird. It's a vicious circle. Crocs seem to be a firm favourite for the summer shoes. Fin likes to wear his with socks, which is a great look. Apparently, this is cool now though. Not so cool when your son will only wear his joggers up to his nipples with it though, which we call his 'Simon Cowell' trousers. It is a strong look; I will give him that.

Another in the long list of contradictions is they hate being touched, but also enjoy the pressure of another person. It is really hard to explain but they don't enjoy cuddles, it needs to be more of a squeeze. Poppy will literally push her head against mine until it actually hurts. And Fin needs constant touch, but his way of doing it is to simply beat us up all the time (I am talking play fighting, not actually beating us), which again, bloody hurts! It is lovely when your children show their affection to you by punching you or squashing your face.

I can't tell you the number of times that Poppy has created something using our rubbish, plants and cutlery that she has found around the house. To me it looks a lot like trash, I won't lie, but then she explains it to me, and I am blown away as I can then see exactly what she has made, and it's actual art. Fin isn't the most creative but he does manage to store facts about things that he is interested in. I won't need to read all the information when walking around the Sea Life Centre, as I have Fin next to me telling me everything you could know about the sea creatures.

I have to say, I love their quirks, and it is one of the reasons I would never want to change them. As much as they struggle at times with their diagnosis, it can also bring out such a funny and incredible way of thinking. I don't want people to think it is all fun and games, but it isn't all doom and gloom either. It's a mixture.

For example, a lot of children are scared of bugs and spiders, but not to the extent that Poppy is. It has been really hard to get Poppy into the garden this summer. She is terrified of the bugs out there, and if she spots the smallest spider, it will lead to a horrific meltdown, where she is almost sick with fear. It is horrible to see, as she is actually shaking with fear. I am so worried about the day that she sees a big spider in the house. We have been lucky so far, but I know soon it will happen. The contradiction here though is she is fascinated by bugs. It's almost like a love-hate relationship with them. We have had to make many homes for woodlouse and snails. Maybe they are more predictable than other bugs, but even flies will at times scare her and other times not. We went to a café only yesterday, and she called the fly in there 'Angela' and Angela had some lunch with us. So, it is confusing. Our kids really do like to keep us on our toes.

Even now, after 11 years, I still struggle at times to know what has triggered a meltdown. I think we continue learning every day. Over time, the thing I have got better at is spotting a meltdown as it begins. I can almost see their face change and the body language. To an outsider, they probably look fine, but I think as parents, you begin to notice it more. It's like I can feel a shift in the mood, and it immediately fills me with anxiety, as I know what is about to come. Some people have said to me in the past that offering them an ice lolly can help to calm them down. I am not sure if this works or not. I feel I would just end up having a lolly thrown in my face, as I can't imagine they will be very happy with me offering them some food while they are beside themselves and struggling to breath.

It reminds me of when I was in labour with Fin. I was just approaching 9cm dilated at home, but Terry didn't believe me; he thought the contractions were too far apart. Typical man, going by the book rather than actually listening to his wife. I was in absolute agony and thought I was going to pass out with the pain. I kept telling him to call the nurses and tell them we are coming in whether they like it or not, but Terry thought he had a better idea. Do you know what he did? He offered me a bloody cheese sandwich. I am in the most horrific pain of my life, feeling like my insides are being ripped out of me, pouring with sweat while pacing up and down our room, trying to find an escape to this agony I was in and my hero of a husband offers me a cheese sandwich. I think it was very lucky for him that I was in too much pain to have the strength to punch him, as I definitely would have done if I could.

My advice to people when dealing with meltdowns is to just try to ride it out.

It sounds like useless advice, but I feel that there is not much you can do, and it is your child simply expressing their feelings. It is hard to not be afraid of them though when they feel so intense and at times, can hurt themselves or others. It is one of the main reasons that I get nervous letting other people look after them, as I don't know how others would cope in this situation. People always seem terrified and, in these times, I feel you need to be quite strong and try to take control of the situation.

That is why we don't really have anyone that can look after them. Before my mum became a carer to my dad, she would sometimes have either Fin or Pops, but I really don't think I could trust anyone else to have them. Not because I don't trust the person, but it is just so much to think about and worry about that I really don't think I would enjoy my time away anyway. If you ever do get any offers of help, you feel like you need to write down a whole schedule of all the possibilities as even we never know how a day out will go and even we, as the parents, don't know if something is going to trigger them that day or not, and how to deal with it. So, it becomes an essay trying to think of every possible outcome that you need to warn people about, and it goes like this . . .

You want to take them to the park? That sounds great, thank you. They may love it there, but not if there are too many people. Hopefully it will be warm enough but not too hot, as they don't like the sun in their eyes. I hope it doesn't rain though, as they won't cope with getting wet, so maybe take a change of clothes. Be prepared for a fight though while trying to get it on them as they hate getting dressed, and they will probably try to take off their shoes the minute you get there. If you think the ground is OK, just let them run around with bare feet but be careful if they cut themselves, as they won't let you put a plaster on. They will go into a meltdown if they hurt at all, and it's very likely they will fall over, as they always do within half an hour of us getting anywhere. They will then refuse to walk any further if they hurt themselves, so maybe take the buggy. But you will battle with them to keep them strapped into the buggy, as they will try to escape the whole time, but you will need that for when they need to eat as otherwise, they will run off constantly.

You also need to take their safe food snacks with you, as they probably won't eat anything from the café, but don't let them see that they sell ice creams, or they will want it straight away and won't understand why you say no to them. Actually, it's probably best to just get them the ice cream or they will throw a fit. Don't let them choose which one though, as they will likely choose one they don't like. Also, ask if they can put it in a tub for them as they will freak out if their hands get sticky. Take some baby wipes with you just in case, especially if they need the toilet as they don't like the feeling of toilet paper still. Make sure you take them to the toilet when you first arrive, or they will wet themselves halfway round. Also take them into the disabled one as the hand dryers will cause a meltdown. And definitely avoid the gift shop – they have no concept of money and will just expect you to buy everything for them. Though it's probably worth taking some fidget toys with you for the day in case there is any queuing, as they will get really distressed. Maybe find out if the place offers a queue pass because of this and take the sunflower lanyards* to show they need this assistance. I am afraid they won't actually wear them though as they don't like the feeling, so you will need to keep them on you. Other than that, have a great day . . . And we wonder why no one offers to help.

Top Tips

☆ *Get headphones for yourself so you can still enjoy your music while they listen to theirs.*

☆ *It can be hard to trust people enough to let them look after the kids and believe it will all go well, but try to find a way – you need a break.*

☆ *Forget about having a show home and have a home that makes your life easier by keeping the kids happy.*

---

* Sunflower lanyards are a way to signal you have a hidden disability. See hdsunflower.com.

Chapter Eight

PEACE BEGINS WHERE EXPECTATIONS END

If you have searched any mum groups or social media about autism after the diagnosis, you may find a lot of people talking about the parents grieving. Unless you have been through this yourself, I guess that turn of phrase may seem strange as no one has actually died.

I know, in hindsight, I definitely went through a grieving process. Funnily enough though not really after the diagnosis but more along different stages we get to in their life.

The first one was after having Fin, and I think a lot of it was down to the postnatal depression. This wasn't anything to do with being a SEN parent, but just becoming a parent in general. It was about saying goodbye to our old life as a couple. We only ever had to worry about ourselves, just popping to the shops was easy, grab a bag and go. Now, it was making sure the baby was fed beforehand, packing nappies, dummies, muslins, baby wipes, setting up the pram and making sure he was wrapped up in there. All of this just to head over to Tesco to get some bread. Our whole world had been turned upside down, and it was now all about following routines, getting no sleep, feeding and changing bums, and it wasn't fun.

How could I not have expected this though? We wanted to have a baby. For some reason, I had in my head, our old life, and a baby. Every scenario was as it was then, but with a baby (a sleeping baby I might add). So, it was my ignorance that contributed to it, but can you ever really be prepared for the chaos a child brings? What else in life is absolutely mandatory and yet so tiresome and difficult?

But becoming a SEN parent brought a whole different type of grief with it. Once you have adjusted to being a parent, you begin picturing life again with this little child you have. You start to imagine their dreams for them, all the places you want to take them, all the foods you want them to try, groups you would like them to join and even looking as far ahead as what they may be when they are older. Will they get married?

It is something I think most of us parents do naturally. How many times have we looked at our toddler's awful artwork and said, 'Oh, look. She's going to be a little artist when she's older,' or sticking your child in a funny T-shirt that says, 'Future prime minister.' We can't help but plan their future, as really that's a huge part of being a parent. Trying to give our little people opportunities that we never had, and hoping they will do a lot better than we did. Until we are suddenly stopped in our tracks and our dreams are very abruptly put on hold as we are told their future is going to look very different from what we had planned.

It is like someone has taken all those dreams you had and torn them up. It took me a long time to understand it. I eventually came to the conclusion that it isn't because you want to change your child, or are grieving for the child you never had, it is that you are grieving for all the opportunities your child has had taken from them.

Every child born into this world is innocent and every child deserves the same shot at life as anyone else. Sadly, this will never be the case as not everyone is created equal. Some have wealth on their side, some have skin colour on their side, some have health on their side and some are simply born neurotypical.

People may think they don't have to miss out on anything if we don't allow it. No place can discriminate and say no child with disabilities allowed, but it actually happens all the time, just a little more discreetly than this. There are very few holiday clubs and after school groups that will take SEN children, as they don't have the number of teachers available; and if places offer quiet sessions, they are usually at ridiculous times, if at all. Let's face it, a lot of places don't even offer wheelchair access, which I think is disgusting, so how on earth can we expect places to cater for people with hidden disabilities when they can't even for physical disabilities?

The hardest thing is, we get to see all these missed opportunities every day. Some of us have lost more than others. I am lucky that my children can join in with Halloween and Christmas celebrations, we get to go trick or treating and decorate the tree. Yes, we have the odd wobble here and there with the change of routine, but we can still enjoy some moments. Whereas, I have friends who are not able to join in these events at all as the change is too much for their child. Some can't decorate the house, can't open presents and can't go door to door collecting sweets. They laugh it off at times, 'at least it saves us some money', but I can see through their smile. I can see the hurt because I feel it too but for different things.

One of the moments of grief that came out of nowhere was my children attending different schools. I didn't even realise that it was something that I longed for until it was lost. I sobbed. I had subconsciously pictured them being together: Poppy having her older brother there when she first started so she had someone to look out for her, sibling pictures together for the class photos. I am still unsure why it matters so much to me and wonder if it is because I was an only child until the age of 15. I never experienced having a sibling at school and was jealous of all my friends who did. I hated school so much and I guess it would have kind of been like a support blanket having my family there with me to get through it.

Again, it's looking at things with rose-tinted glasses, as I am sure in reality, Poppy and Fin would have completely ignored each other the whole time they were there anyway, or possibly one would have tried to kill the other. From a selfish point of view though, it would have been a hell of a lot nicer to just do one school run instead of two.

An unexpected one is WhatsApp. Yes, the dreaded school mum WhatsApp group. Mainstream WhatsApp group chats can be a huge trigger in my experience. Obviously, all the people in the group chat are parents of your child's peers. Everything they do is a reminder of what your child is not doing. I remember them talking about Valentine's Day. It was such a small thing, but it hit me like a ton of bricks. One of the boys was taking one of the girls from class on a date. He had bought her a rose and a card and was taking her to the cinema, obviously with the mums taking them. I couldn't comprehend it because Fin was not even close to being at that stage. He doesn't even talk to girls yet, taking them on a date just wouldn't even enter his head. It was just another thing that confirmed how even though these kids are in the same class, they are years apart mentally.

The chats continued talking about after school clubs and football teams. Something my kids would never be part of. Poppy isn't actually allowed to go to any after school clubs, even if she wanted to, as there are not enough TAs available to look after the SEN children. I am grateful that she doesn't want to go to them, as I don't think I would have the heart to tell her she can't because she has a disability.

And it isn't just groups they miss out on. It is parties and sleepovers. All the things you would expect children to love. Parties are usually too overwhelming for them. We have been to many, even our own. I insisted that Fin had parties when he was younger, as I thought it was the thing to do. Not realising that it was actually the worst thing I could do to him. Hey, my shy, antisocial child who likes everything to remain the same, I am going to organise loads of people to come to our house, make lots of noise and disrupt the routine of your day and completely embarrass you by us all singing to you while giving you a cake. How does that sound? It went about as well as you could expect. Fin hid in his room the whole time, while we entertained lots of other children we didn't really care about.

However, Poppy was a little different; she didn't shy away from parties. She just acted like she wasn't really there. We did a joint party for her when she started school, we hired out a hall and had a bouncy castle, bowls of crisps, balloons, soft play mats.

This one felt a little different as it was full of autistic children from Poppy's school, and they were all ignoring each other as much as Poppy was ignoring them. All except my friend's little boy, he is nonverbal and loves to grab hair. Poppy was on the bouncy castle with him and had her hair down. I think you know where I am going with this. Yep, he latched on to it and wouldn't let go. All I heard was a child screaming like they were on fire and knew instantly it was Poppy. With a McDonald's burger in one hand, I clambered on to the bouncy castle to try to release his grip. During this, my Auntie (who is somehow completely oblivious to all the screaming) decided it was a great time for a picture and was calling me and Poppy to smile and say cheese for the camera. I still haven't seen that picture to this day, but it probably isn't one for the family photo album.

It took a while, but eventually she calmed down and when she did, it was time for Fin to start as he had now had enough. He was becoming more and more stressed out with the noise and chaos, so we had to remove him from the situation completely and take him to a quiet room where my mum sat with him.

And this, my friends, is why we no longer do parties.

You have to keep an eye out, as sometimes the small things you notice hit the hardest. I went to a camping site and met some other families with autistic children. I thought this would finally be a place I could fit in, as everyone would be understanding (which they were) and in the same situation. But as it began to get dark, and we sat around the fire pit, Fin could no longer cope with being there and wanted his bedtime routine in place, meaning we had to go and sleep in our tent from around 8pm. I could hear all the others outside still chatting and laughing and I felt so alone. This was a group of autistic families, and I couldn't even join in there. What hope was there for us to ever be able to go out again? The bedtime routine has been such a tough one, as even though he can still be a nightmare to get off to sleep, he is bound by the routine and if it changes slightly, he gets so distressed.

Of course, there are times that I would like to go out with my friends. I rarely do at all but even my one night out every couple of months causes so much disruption that I wonder if it is even worth it to be honest.

I often take the dog for a walk over a field near us at the weekends, I see the football matches going on and all the parents standing on the sideline cheering their children on, and I wonder how that feels, to see your children performing, winning a game or dancing in a show. We have tried several groups with the kids, but it was too hard. Fin tried karate but he couldn't cope with the shouting and the strict rules, and I tried to take Poppy to ballet classes. It started off OK and she was actually following the teacher but as the weeks went on, she became more reluctant to join in and, in typical Poppy fashion, would be on her own agenda and I would spend most of the lesson chasing her around the back of the class. I imagine it was quite a funny sight, with all the lovely little ballerinas sitting perfectly still and listening to the teacher, while some crazy lady and her feral child (who is currently pulling out her bun) are darting around the hall, the little girl giggling while the mum looks out of breath and sweaty.

It's not just groups that I think about, its concerts too. Oh, to take the kids to a concert would be a dream come true. Obviously, the noise would be a huge barrier for them, but the other thing would be finding music they actually enjoy that isn't from a cartoon. This is something that I really do struggle with: I would love for them to enjoy some things that we enjoy. I know lots of kids love the Masked Singer and X Factor and Britain's Got Talent and I'm a celeb, get me out of here. OK, now I am just naming all the shows I love. I have tried many times to get the kids to watch something, I have even skipped to the fun bits that I think they would like such as dogs doing the dancing and people eating bugs, but they just don't pay attention to it. It drives me nuts! How can you still pay attention to episode 12 of SpongeBob that you have probably now seen 85 times and still watch it like it's the first time you are seeing it, but not be interested in someone eating a spider that is REAL? And they won't just accept any old cartoon either. Even Disney doesn't get played in the house anymore, which I find absolutely unacceptable. But it is so hard to get them to watch anything new at all now. We have to put a new film on in the background at least ten times before they will start to enjoy it, which means most films we go to see at the cinema they don't enjoy. I still will try every week to get them back to Disney though, I won't give up. My dream is to go to Disneyland one day; whether I am dragging them around it or not, I am determined we will do it.

It is amazing the things that can hurt sometimes. It

sounds silly to outsiders but sometimes it's totally under-standable, like only a week ago, we had Fin's year 6 leavers' do and we were saying goodbye to not only primary but to mainstream school, so as you can imagine, I was a com-plete mess. I can't describe to you this overwhelming feeling of loss. I am obviously ecstatic that he has got into a SEN school finally, and this is thanks to my lawyer friend, Hannah, who is a SEN solicitor. Without her mafia style persistence, I don't think we would have been accepted, but the council couldn't help but allow it when she pointed out all the problems with Fin's EHCP. I was slightly con-cerned that at one point they may end up with a horse's head in their bed, but luckily it didn't get that far. As much as I was delighted, it still hurt to say goodbye to main-stream. It was a weird feeling to finally accept that this isn't and was never the place for him.

I have definitely saved some money though on school trips and discos and the costliest trip of all – the year 6 resi-dential. This was another thing that broke my heart a little. I saw all the information coming through from the school about it, go ape, bowling, pizzas and a school sleepover camping out and with a heavy heart I knew he wouldn't go. Being his final year at primary school, I don't want him to miss any opportunities there that he will never get back, but I also can't force him to do these things. I just wish he would try at times. And as for Pops, I doubt she will ever do residential either. I don't think this is something they would offer at a SEN school. I can't imagine it anyway.

Even just watching her sports day showed the kind of chaos it would be. Kids running everywhere, some throw-ing items, some not joining in at all. Screaming, laughing, crying. It was great, don't get me wrong. I love that they can just be themselves but a sleepover with them all – hell no. The teachers definitely don't get paid enough for that! I am grateful though that I was able to see Poppy run in her sports day the first year of school, something that I don't get to see with Fin. The last few years he has refused to do it, and I don't blame him at all. I hated every minute of it, but this year Poppy refused for the first time too and I felt so bloody sad about it. I thought Poppy would always be my one that didn't care what others thought, but slowly she seems to be becoming more self-aware and not wanting to do as much as she used to. Even with all the other SEN children, she was the one to refuse to do it and once again, we are not part of something. I will never push them to do something they hate though and especially with something like sports day. If you are not good at sports, it is basically a day to show you up for being shit at running. How is this good for anyone's self-esteem? Can you imagine if they did this every year with Maths and English? We are going to make you stand in front of the whole school and parents and we will find out who is the cleverest and who is the thickest child here! I personally think sports day should be optional, whether you have SEN needs or not. So, in actual fact, maybe not being in something at all is better than being last and being miserable.

I will never forget Fin's first sports day. It was the egg and spoon race, and they were told by the teachers to not drop the egg. For an autistic child who takes things literally, he heard, you must not drop the egg. The other children heard – run and if you drop it, just pick it up again and keep running. So, you can imagine how the race went.

Fin was last, by a mile. He was walking at the rate of a tortoise, holding his egg and spoon with such care, as if it were a delicate baby that he must look after. The other children had all finished, and he was still not even at the halfway mark. I began cheering for him, and then some of the other parents joined in too, as we patiently waited for him to cross the finish line, which took him probably about 15 minutes. Tears ran down my face with pride and love for this boy who did exactly as he was told. He may have lost but in my eyes, he was the winner. He was the only one that followed the rules, the others were cheats. I mean, they were only around the age of five, but still, they were cheating. Technically, he won as he didn't drop the egg.

Seriously. He fucking won. Fight me.

Getting back to the leaver's assembly, they played a video that showed all the photos of the children from when they started school right through to today. The other mums were crying, reminiscing on all the things their children had done. I was crying but for different reasons. I was crying for my little boy who has been the outsider his whole life. I cried for the boy who had struggled to fit in. I cried for the boy who wasn't in any of the photos for the sleepovers as he couldn't cope with it. I cried for the boy who was standing in front of me, trying desperately to join in but being ignored. I think letting go of mainstream school was the final goodbye to the life that we had pictured.

But it's not all bad. As well as all the school activities, think of the money we save on clubs and groups out of school. Actually, that isn't strictly true as we have taken the kids to SEN sessions for swimming and cycling instead, which cost about three times the amount of any clubs they would join. These sessions were worth every penny though, to see them riding a bike after years and years of not being able to. So, sometimes dreams do come true, just a bit later than others, Fin learned to ride a bike at the age of ten and I couldn't be prouder. In fact, maybe I am even prouder than the parents of a four-year-old that learned as we have had to wait so much longer to see it.

I wonder often how things will be for them as they get older. There are some autistic children that will never get to go to a nightclub, get drunk with friends and needing picking up at 3am. Maybe this is a blessing, at least we won't have the worry of them getting their drink spiked or being beaten up, but it still feels like another milestone that is missed. Or is it for the in-between kids? The children like Fin, possibly Poppy. Maybe he will go to a nightclub, the noise and people would be too much for him surely? But if he wants to fit in with friends maybe he would force himself to go. If he did go though, he would be vulnerable. Would people notice he was different and single him out? Would they see him as weak and an easy target? Or Poppy as well. I dread to think of letting go enough to allow her to do these things. Of course, I can't hold her back and stop her, that wouldn't be fair, but I definitely won't get any sleep that night. In fact, I am pretty sure I would sit outside in my car waiting for her to exit the whole time. So even if they do get to do something that neurotypicals do, do they ever really get to experience them in the same way as others when they are so vulnerable still?

Even though some of these things leave you with a feeling a sadness that you won't ever get to experience them with your child, there are so many things that we do get to experience instead; it can just take our mindset a little while to shift into what our life looks like now compared to what our expectations were.

There are things that neurotypical parents may never feel, like seeing your child come alive when splashing in water or playing with bubbles. They may get these moments when they had toddlers, seeing their faces light up as they play but those moments are gone quickly. We get to relive these moments for years. We get to watch their eyes sparkle as they see things we don't in those bubbles. Also, as I drop Fin off at school, he is still waving to me as he walks in, he is in year 6 and the other kids are too embarrassed to be waving to their mum now. They are too cool, but he doesn't care, because I am still his safe place, and I hope I always will be their safe place. I feel that in some ways our children stay children for longer and keep their innocence for longer and that can only ever be a good thing. Growing up is shit. Learning about the horrible things in this world is shit. Even though people say having children with disabilities must be an awful thing, they always talk about the things they can't do and all the things they are missing and how much harder life is. But I no longer view it that way, I think of how much our life has changed for the better since having them and I know they bring joy to others too. Their teachers love their funny ways as much as we do. People say that autistic people don't have empathy, but I think this couldn't be further from the truth. In particular, the empathy they feel for animals is one of the reasons I think that the world is a better place having autistic people in it. I sometimes think we are the lucky ones.

Top Tips

☆ *Grief will fade and be replaced by something so much better.*

☆ *It is perfectly OK and normal to feel sad that life wasn't how you expected.*

☆ *Stop looking back and start planning forward.*

☆ *This too shall pass. It always does.*

Chapter Nine

PDA – POPPY DOESN'T AGREE

For anyone who doesn't know, PDA stands for pathological demand avoidance. I like to call it Poppy Doesn't Agree or, sometimes, Pretty Damn Annoying. The only way I can explain it from our experience is when they need to control everything. It is usually due to their anxiety, and it makes everyday tasks really difficult for them, even impossible at times. PDA means you have to parent and teach in a completely different way, as any demands placed on them, however inconsequential, become a crippling obstacle.

We are still unsure if Poppy has it or not, as it is actually not recognised as a diagnosis in Kent, where we live. I find this unbelievable. We could move to a different county, and she could get a diagnosis. PDA doesn't just leave you the minute you walk into Kent. Or come on like an attack of diarrhoea as soon as you cross the border.

I think the local authority believe if they just ignore it enough, it will go away. I wish that was the case with my bills coming through every month, or the potholes in my road.

As with a lot of things about autism, I had never heard of PDA before Poppy started school. At school, her teacher suggested it to me as a possible barrier for Poppy, and I looked into it further. One of the signs of PDA was spending a lot of time in role play and pretend.

Now this was an absolutely huge flag for Poppy as about 90 per cent of her days are spent in a make-believe world. At the moment, she lives in Bikini Bottom – it is SpongeBob's home in case you didn't know – the issue is, we have to live there too. I have to be careful where I sit in the lounge in case I sit on one of the SpongeBob characters I can't see, I have to strap SpongeBob in with a seat belt on car journeys and we have to make up a place for him at the dinner table as well as some actual food.

I tried to give him some make-believe invisible food, but Poppy looked at me in absolute disgust and said, 'There is no food there!' Of course, how stupid of me trying to give SpongeBob, the fictional character off the TV, a plate of pretend food.

Her teachers even have to set up a seat for him during circle time. I can only imagine the other kids wondering if their teacher has gone mad because she is always setting up a spare seat for an invisible person and won't let them sit there!

I am saying this light-heartedly, and we absolutely love the imagination she has, but we do believe now that a lot of this is an escape technique and a coping mechanism. Poppy can't cope with the demands put on her in this world, so she disappears into a world that she can control, which has no demands on her there. This means that at school, for example, she is in SpongeBob world most of the time, and her teachers can't reach her there.

It is frustrating because she is so clever. Her teacher and I know she can read and write, but she just refuses to do it on demand. We have to wait until she chooses to do it or is triggered to do so by the events in her world.

As such, our parenting and teaching need to be redesigned in a way that forces her back into our world while making sure she still feels in control of it, otherwise we just lose her again.

Going through her workbooks did make me laugh, and I felt for the poor teachers trying to force her to do her work as there really was no hope. The worksheets of math questions would be answered simply with SpongeBob pictures and throughout the book it stated 'Poppy participated in her own way', which I know means she refused to fucking do it and did as she pleased.

Seriously, no wonder they give you just a rubbish leaflet at the autism assessment – how do you teach this shit? Every demand needs to be put to her in a clever way to make her feel she has made the decision.

It is time to brush her teeth, the worst thing you could say is 'Poppy, you need to go and brush your teeth now.' You may as well pin her down and shove a toothbrush in her mouth. It needs to be framed as a casual question instead: 'Poppy, do you fancy brushing your teeth before you have your toast or after?'

Simple. Nailed it.

Yeah, not so much. When she has made the decision to do it after her toast, you then need to remind her again in a way that doesn't sound like a demand. 'Poppy, you said you wanted to brush your teeth now, so do you want to stand up while doing it or sit down?'

This works some of the time, but being blunt, it is fucking exhausting. Even the part of actually brushing the teeth is hard enough, but it is even hard work getting there. She will take her own sweet time. She will crawl (literally) up the stairs, stopping on every step while we continue to call her.

Now just to confuse things even more, if she does brush her teeth without any fuss, you would automatically want to praise her to encourage her to behave like this again next time. In actual fact, praise can be seen as an expectation to some PDAers and they actually hate it. They feel that because you have cheered for them having brushed their teeth, you are now going to expect this every day, and this is now a demand again. I have learned to instead praise the actual activity rather than them, the person. So, I would say something along the lines of 'Wow, those teeth have had a really good brush. They look so lovely and clean' instead of 'Well done, you brushed your teeth so well!'

It is at the end of this kind of spiritually and mental-draining ordeal that I think back to days before kids. You remember, right? Lie-ins at the weekend, any TV programmes we wanted to watch, last-minute weekends away, lunch with friends and drunk taxi rides home ... actually, this is quite depressing, where am I going with this? Ah yes.

Fuck my life.

I never in a million years thought I would spend an hour every morning negotiating with a miniature version of myself about brushing her sodding teeth. I must admit I got desperate once and actually showed her pictures off the internet of people's rotting, black teeth. This back-fired as it made her sick and then she couldn't sleep with the fear of teeth falling out. So, like I said previously, fuck my life.

Until your child has PDA, I don't think you appreciate

how many individual tasks there are in life. It is much like when you break a bone, you don't realise how much you actually use that bone for everything you do! We have always called Poppy a sloth as she takes so long to do things, but this is just very clever tactics. She is controlling the narrative again, by taking her time to do anything we ask. If she has done it in her own time, she has exerted some control over it.

This does mean we are late for everything. And I mean everything!

Just between you and I, I used to be late for everything before having kids anyway, but at least I have a good excuse now. I am sorry I am late; my daughter took an hour to crawl across the floor like a sea cucumber because I asked her to put her shoes on. Once she had crawled across at a snail's pace, she then decided to put the shoes on her hands instead of her feet. When I reminded her they needed to go on her feet, she then put them each on the wrong foot on purpose, so in the end I gave in and did it for her.

Being late is obviously annoying for everyone - the people waiting for us as well as ourselves, but when it is for something important then it becomes a real problem. Such as when we were going on holiday and realised we had exactly two minutes until the gate closed but we still needed to walk to it. Terry and Fin ran ahead, I am not sure how this would have helped, or what they were going to do when getting there. I imagined Terry shouting, 'Stop the plane!!!' or maybe distracting the people working in the airport lounge so they didn't close the doors. Possibly him and Fin were going to break into a dance while me and Poppy snuck past. Who knows? But anyway, they left us to do whatever it is they intended to do, and I had to some-how get Poppy to move quicker without her thinking I was making her.

So, the first thing I tried was to turn it into a game, of course involving SpongeBob. I tried to say that we were being chased by SpongeBob, but she soon put me right and told me that he wasn't doing that, stop being ridicu-lous mum, he's literally right here. I then tried just telling her the truth, the plane was going to go without us, but this seemed to slow her down more. And then it came to me, the answer to our problems. I told her to go really slow. Yes, I am an absolute bloody genius. I kept telling her to stop and she would run ahead giggling, little cow! She started going quicker and we just made it. I have to warn you though, this method doesn't always work. Kids are clever and she sometimes knows exactly what I am up to, and they play us as much as we play them. If this happens, there is only one option. You have to bloody drag them kicking and screaming.

A lot of times I ask Poppy to do something, she will actually fake an injury. We need to brush her hair but all of a sudden, she has hurt her leg and can't possibly move from where she is. Even things that she will want to do become a demand if I tell her to do it. I could tell her that we are going to Disneyland for the day, and she will have unlimited ice cream but if I ask her in the wrong way, she will say she doesn't want to go.

Obviously for Poppy, who has sensory issues with eating, food can become a huge demand, so we have to tread very carefully with this one. We always offer lots of different options and she seems to get on the best with picky food because of this. This does unfortunately create a lot of wastage but that is one of the only things our dog, Frankie, is useful for: clearing up the leftovers; as with most Labradors, he is literally a walking stomach. I have also found that letting her make her own food gives her some control with it too, making her toast means she is far more likely to eat her breakfast in the morning. Again, it means we are horribly late though. I think the most painful thing I have ever had to watch in my life is my children spreading butter on toast. If you don't know what this looks like, imagine a blind monkey with only thumbs trying to tie a shoelace. A close second to the most painful things in the world to watch is Poppy actually eating the toast. This, I believe, is another control thing. Telling you she eats slowly would be an understatement. She takes roughly an hour to eat one bit of toast. We can't rush her as she will then refuse to eat, and she actually needs to eat in order to live. Even though, I am concerned she may turn into a chicken nugget one day as her body must surely now be at least 90 per cent nugget.

When raising children with PDA you hear a lot of negatives, but these can be positives too. Head strong. This is something that people usually say in a negative way, but I don't think it is. Head strong children go on to be people that lead others. Defiant. They are the ones that are not afraid to question things they think are wrong; they are the ones who make a stand to change the world. And I think this will be Pops. She won't take shit from anyone.

So, once you think you have learned everything about autism, PDA comes along and slaps you in the face and you need to unlearn everything. The issue is, there is no manual or course you can go on. You just have to somehow ride the wave, do your best and hope for the best. Eventually you will reach your destination. It may just take you a few years instead of a few hours, and a hell of a lot of negotiating with your little PDAer.

Top Tips

☆ *Help your PDAer to feel in control as much as possible. For example, let them choose their outfit or how they have their hair.*

☆ *Give yourself extra time for negotiations.*

☆ *Use your child's special interest to help them with everyday tasks.*

☆ *Try to not overly praise.*

Chapter Ten

IS IT JUST ME OR ADHD?

As many of us know now, autism is often in the genes. It is funny the amount of neurodivergent people you can spot once you start looking around you and especially in the family. But before I began to look at my parent's traits, I first needed to start looking at myself and I could see so much of myself in my children that it all started to fall into place as to why we had not one, but two autistic children.

Terry would often be confused as to why the kids were overreacting to things, whereas I could completely understand why they were beside themselves over something, as I would be overreacting to it too if it happened to me. On the days out when we would take the kids to a farm or maybe a trampoline park, I would be relieved to leave. This would happen even at events that you would assume I would enjoy, such as family parties or a trip to a theme park. The kids would decide they no longer wanted to be there, so we would leave early and as we travelled back home, I would give a sigh of relief that we were going back home. I started to wonder if it was relief as the kids were heading into a meltdown which we caught early or was it in fact that I wanted to go back to my safe place too. On arriving home, I would instantly feel that sense of happiness that we were back in our little bubble again, away from people and away from the rest of the world.

Seeing my children's struggles socially made me look deeper into my emotions surrounding meeting people, and I finally understood what I was feeling. I would be drained after meeting with friends and feel physically and emotionally burnt out. Don't get me wrong, I enjoyed my time with my friends, but when it was done, I didn't want to see another person for at least a week. I craved to be alone. Luckily, I have neurodivergent friends who totally get this too and feel the same about me. However, some friends don't. Some have suggested to me a long weekend away together. Erm, hell no. I did two nights with my friends recently for my 40th and trust me that was enough.

There were about ten of us, which is a lot to take anyway in one go, and we spent two nights together. This may not sound like much, but on the last morning, I couldn't wait to leave them all. I love them to bits, but there is only so much socialising you can do. Plus, just wanting to be back in my own bed and shower in my own shower. I never truly feel comfortable doing this in other places.

... And, of course, I wanted to get home to see the kids ... A bit. Well, I thought I did until the second I got home, when they started fighting with each other and throwing food on the floor, and then socialising for an extra night didn't seem like such a bad idea anymore.

I guess growing up you just assume this is the way that everyone feels, and it is not until you are an outsider looking in at your children, compared to their peers, that you realise this isn't the norm.

I then began to look at myself as a child of their age, and it all added up. I hated sleepovers back then too. I loved them at my own house but going over to other people's houses filled me with dread. I could never sleep properly in a different bed; I never liked their food as it was different to ours at home. Frequently, my parents would be called to come and pick me up because I suddenly felt sick in the night. They must have been delighted to be called out at midnight every time! Sometimes I was actually sick, and I think it was the stress of it all.

At primary school I was painfully shy and didn't ever feel close to anyone. I don't remember ever missing my friends in the school holidays or wanting to spend time with them. I was pretty much an outcast, but I really was happy that way. I try to remind myself of this when I worry about the kids playing alone. I loved to play alone. I remember collecting all the Kinder Egg toys and would sit for hours in my room, playing with them all. If other people were involved, they would have messed up the game, so I was happy to be a loner until I went to secondary school and somehow, I ended up in the popular group.

Don't ask me how, I have no clue how I got there. I am guessing it was probably down to masking at this stage. I was no longer the shy kid; I was quite loud and always bunking school. I became the naughty one. Even though I was giving off this air of confidence, I didn't feel it.

Once again, I felt like I didn't fit. I felt weird and not worthy of anyone, but suddenly had a need to fit in and be liked because that was where I'd ended up. I was constantly chasing the dream of people liking me and getting attention, even though I didn't really want it. I guess some could say that has never really changed as now I look for likes and attention on my social media.

Huh.

Truthfully, it probably is partly that still. The girl who doesn't really believe she is good at anything is still inside me and when people tell me that I am doing a good job or make them laugh, it makes me feel good about who I am. I am trying to learn now though that I don't need people to like me in order to like myself. I don't need validation from others to feel valid. I will keep reminding myself of this, but I do wonder if I had been given a diagnosis at a younger age and the support I needed, would I feel this way or would I have been able to understand myself better? And therefore know there was never anything wrong with me – I was just different and that is OK.

Another big red flag came up. Looking back to primary school again, I had issues with eating. I would barely eat anything that wasn't spaghetti hoops and ham. I was as skinny as a rake and as pale as a ghost, which prompted the teachers to have a word with my mum to say they were concerned. She took me to the doctors. The doctor told her not to worry and if that were the only foods I would eat, she should just give me that.

If anyone out there is going through this with their child barely eating, I would like to give you some hope as I eat practically everything now – so much so that I am overweight. If only I could go back to the ham and spaghetti hoop days, I might get my figure back again.

So, the signs were definitely there in more ways than I even realised. I used to do gymnastics and absolutely loved it. I went every week for years and was gaining more badges until they changed their location. We could still get to the new location, it was only around the corner. The teachers and classes were the same but that was it, it was in a different place, so I refused to go again.

The thing is, it was a different time back then and no one knew as much as they do now. No one helped because no one knew there was any need to help.

For my parents' generation, it was even worse. They would have never picked up on their traits, but I definitely see the traits in them now. My dad has Parkinson's disease and one of the nurses who came to see him mentioned to my mum about him being autistic. My dad has never been a sociable guy, always kept himself to himself and even would come across as rude at times. People often referred to him as very serious as he rarely smiled, and he couldn't cope with change. Totally like Fin! When the nurse said this, it all made sense! My mum, however, has ADHD traits; she can't sit still to save her life and is always distracted in conversations. I will be on the phone to her, talking about my day, and suddenly she will start talking about a man that has been stuck up a mountain for the last three months. When I ask where on earth that came from, she'll say, 'Oh, sorry love, I am just reading this magazine.' She was, of course, known as the daydreamy child when growing up and obsessed with animals, much like Poppy.

I do often wonder how many old people have gone their whole lives not knowing why they were different. There are so many that say they are just 'stuck in their ways' but has this always been the case with them? Can they just not cope with change and like their routine?

Think about it. How many old people do we know

that always go to the bank on a Wednesday at 10am just because that is the day they have to do it? How many times do grandparents grumble about that new restaurant that has opened and is serving all that funny food? I don't know, maybe you just become an old misery as time goes on. I know I certainly am.

I have got to the stage in life where I am now moaning if the bin men are late. For some reason, the bins cause a lot of stress in later life. Which bin day is it? Why has Maureen got her green bin out when it is black bin day? Is she wrong, or am I? Who does the bin cleaning? And don't even get me started on the bin day changes around Christmas time, it's the fucking binpocalypse.

I really could write a book just about bin issues alone.

My elderly neighbour is proof that it is never too old to get diagnosed. He must be in his eighties and got diagnosed with autism only a couple of years ago. Once he told me this, everything made sense. The day we moved into our new home, he abruptly came over to me and said that I must have a lot of money to be able to buy a property, and how much did I pay for the house. I couldn't believe how rude this guy was, he hadn't even said welcome, and we hadn't even opened the door yet. He drove me mad, every time I left the house, I dreaded what he would say to me, as quite often he would tell me things like 'you look rough today' or 'you look like you have put on a bit of weight'. In the end though, I grew to love this weird relationship we had where we could tell each other anything. Many a time I told him that he had pissed me off and to bugger off. It was refreshing. No fakeness. No small talk. Sometimes a bit of honesty is what we all need . . . and the freedom of just telling people to fuck all the way off.

Anyway, back to me figuring out that I could in fact be neurodivergent. The more I read, the more it led me to ADHD, and anyone that knows me would agree. I mentioned early on that I struggle to keep to tasks, and it's true. Half our house is decorated but I never got round to finishing it. And I don't mean half the house as in 50 per cent of the total rooms, I mean 50 per cent of each room. Half the wall painted, half the shelves filled with a theme, colour scheme, etc.

I have many grand ideas of new things I would like to start, hobbies I would like to do, and I do them a couple of times and then move on to something else. It is really frustrating. I would love to live in an organised, mess-free house but I just can't. My home is as chaotic as my head is. Unfinished tasks everywhere, which leaves me feeling overwhelmed a lot.

Terry often says it is like a crime scene when he walks into the house as he can see exactly where I have been and what happened. He can see that the dishwasher is half-emptied; it wasn't finished because I had dropped a plate that was smashed on the floor, but why was the smashed plate in the bin but the small broken pieces still left? She obviously went to get the dustpan and brush from the cupboard as the cupboard door was left open but in doing so, she found the tortoise food and remembered he needed to be fed. The tortoise food though is left on the table next to the open cupboard, this is where she usually fills his bowl, but she hasn't done. Why not? Ah, because the table had the kids' toys on it, so she needed to go and put them away, which is why Terry now finds me in the kid's bedroom hoovering. He said it is like following a breadcrumb trail.

ADHD doesn't just mean I have a messy house though; it also means I have a messy mind. I find I get quite overwhelmed all the time by different dates and appointments. Taking my example of me cleaning, imagine that in your mind too. Every time I go to book something or fill out some paperwork that I needed to do weeks ago, I become distracted with another task. Having kids has made it 100 times worse as before them. Earlier I only had to manage my own appointments. Now, I am juggling my life on top of school appointments, homework, dentist and doctor appointments, DLA paperwork, people's birthdays, fun days out, swimming lessons, updating the kids' wardrobe, buying uniforms and just trying to keep them alive in general. It is a complete muddle. Then I have a meltdown.

Terry is confused. I have begun sobbing because he didn't change the loo roll, but it isn't about that. It never is, it is just the straw that broke the camel's back. The poor guy spends a lot of his time confused as he doesn't have a constant hurricane going off in his head. I asked him what he thinks about before going to sleep and do you know what he said to me? 'Nothing.' Nothing! I didn't even realise that this was an actual thing and that people really can have nothing rolling around in their head. I would love to know what nothing feels like.

I try to prioritise tasks, but I admit, I am sometimes the terrible mum that has forgotten their lunch and non-uniform days before. I feel so awful and even drove back to the school to give it to them. As much as we laugh about these ADHD quirks, it can be a real pain in the arse at times and tiring constantly playing catch-up on urgent tasks.

I am talking like I have been diagnosed and actually I haven't. I have been referred and have been told the waiting list is three years. I was undecided whether to go for a diagnosis or not. I am 40 now and got this far without one, is it needed or is it wasting the doctor's time? I had spoken to others who had received their diagnosis and were now on medication for their ADHD. They told me it had changed their life, and they could now do tasks easily, some had even mentioned that they had come off their antidepressants because of it. Now this is something that I really want. I don't want to be on antidepressants forever and I feel like they are simply masking the real issue anyway. If getting a diagnosis can help me with this and I can possibly get medication to help me not get overwhelmed with everything, then it is worth giving it a go, I guess.

If only I had called the doctor years ago when I first suspected this, but the irony is, I didn't because I probably have ADHD and many times, I forgot to do it or just got distracted. I wonder how many people have undiagnosed ADHD because they just never got round to calling the doctor to make that referral.

So here I am, 40 years old and just starting to understand who I am. Isn't it crazy that you can spend your whole life looking in the mirror, but it isn't until we bring our little people into the world that we truly see ourselves?

Top Tips

☆ *It is never too late to get a diagnosis – arrange that appointment now.*

☆ *Looking at your family history with autism or ADHD can sometimes help the diagnosis of your children.*

☆ *Keep hold of any school reports you had to show the doctor at your assessment.*

☆ *List everything that you struggle with and try to come up with solutions of how to make these struggles a little better for you in life.*

Chapter Eleven

WHEN YOU NEED TO BOOK ANOTHER HOLIDAY AFTER YOUR HOLIDAY

I used to think holidays were a time to get away from it all and relax, let your body recover from being over-worked all the time. That was before I had kids. Holidays with kids are anything but relaxing, and usually require you to book another holiday immediately after to recover from this one.

I don't come back from holidays with a renewed vigour for parenting, I come back with the taste of freedom still fresh in my mouth and a deep-seated feeling that life should be all beaches and margaritas.

As I said in my introduction, this year was the first year we had ever taken the kids abroad. Most of our holidays before now were in the Isle of Wight, which I really recommend by the way. One of the best things I found about the Isle of Wight was practically all the days out will give you a pass for a week! I believe every single farm, theme park and zoo should be doing this in the UK. Obviously, it is great for the days that it is pouring with rain, you haven't lost any money as you can simply go the next day or the day after, but it is especially good for having autistic children.

I realise this is starting to sound like a travel guide... don't worry, you haven't accidentally picked up a brochure from Thomas Cook.

You never know how the day will go, and sometimes you can only be somewhere for an hour before they decide they want to leave. This way it doesn't matter as you can just go back again at no extra cost. One of the places we loved to go was Black Gang Chine; Fin particularly loved it there because of the dinosaurs. When he was in his dinosaur obsession phase, one day was not enough for him. He kept wanting to go back and so we did throughout the week!

This year we felt they were old enough to try to take them further and try something new, which Fin was not pleased about.

His main worry was that the plane was going to crash and told this to us every day leading up to holiday. How likely is it? What are the statistics? Do we all die if the plane crashes? What if it crashes in the water?

This made me bloody nervous too and I have never been a nervous flyer before, but someone constantly making you look up examples of air disasters can take the hardest of hearts.

We had saved enough money to actually do it. We had saved for many months leading up to it, and it was time. When I say we saved money, we saved enough to go to Benidorm, not the Bahamas. But Benidorm seemed the perfect place as a trial for them anyway. It was only a two-hour plane journey and Benidorm is very English. It is pretty much England but hotter. We thought at least the food would probably be a safe bet for them as again, it's very English.

We tried to prepare the kids as much as possible: We read books about flying and used social stories to inform them what the plan was, what the process would be, what to expect at each stage. Fin was not any help at all with keeping things calm for Poppy, due to catastrophising and worrying about everything that may possibly go wrong.

Considering Fin had been scaring Poppy leading up to it, especially about the plane crashing, it turned out that Poppy was a much better flyer than Fin and didn't really give a shit about it at all. Saying that, even Fin was fine until the plane started to descend and he suffered the dreaded popping of the ears. We were worried about this before-hand as we know how sensitive he is to things like this, so we packed lots of sucky sweets and had his ear defend-ers, but he got himself into a state and then wouldn't calm enough to actually suck the sweets. It's OK though, people couldn't really hear his cries over the top of Poppy shouting, 'It's making my willy go funny.' I think she meant to say her tummy.

Soon we landed and grabbed our luggage to go and find our transfer bus. And this is where the real hell began. The hotel was about a 40-minute drive from the airport but because of all the people being dropped off on the way, the journey became over two hours and, of course, as luck would have it, our hotel was the last stop. Fin was done by this point; he had had enough and couldn't cope.

The anxiety from it all, the travelling, the ear popping and now being stuck on a coach led to a huge meltdown. He was beside himself, head butting the seat in front while begging for it to be over. It is heartbreaking to see him like that and reminds me of how many struggles he has but keeps in, we only see them when they boil over and pour out. There was nothing we could do but wait and try to calm and reassure him.

Now I look back, I can laugh at the situation. There was a group of young lads on there going on their first boys' holiday together and they were obviously very excited and wanted to chat to us. They were completely oblivious of Fin having a breakdown and kept trying to chat to us about their hotel and places to go out. They were really lovely and friendly but seriously, read the fucking room!

When we finally got to our hotel, we entered our room to find that the air con unit was hanging off the wall and making a loud banging noise while it was on. All we wanted to do was get settled and get all the kids' toys out for them, but we had to wait around to change rooms. At this point, I started to think we had made the biggest mistake ever, why on earth would we do this to ourselves? Once we changed rooms, it didn't get much better either. When we booked our hotel, we requested a family one, where the bedrooms were separate. However, the only room they had available to change us to was one that was open plan and all in the same room together. What's the problem with this you ask? Well, firstly, the kids sleep with so many sensory lights on it is like you are in the middle of a fucking rave, or as my mum would say, 'It's like Blackpool illuminations,' and secondly, they have to have white noise on very loud, so not only will we be blinded by the lights throughout the night, it will also sound like we are in a fucking wind tunnel.

The next day though, watching the kids playing in the splash park with the sun beating down, made all the worries disappear. They were loving every minute. Fin constantly laid face down with his head in the water, enjoying the sensory sensation, as much as it freaked us and the lifeguards out, as he did resemble a dead body floating. Poppy would spend her time fixated with a little pineapple that would fill up with water and then splash down. She loved trying to put balls in it and got so excited every time it tipped up. I knew then that we had made the right decision.

Throughout the week, the kids came out of themselves more. Fin even went up and ordered a drink by himself. He would never have done this in England before but for some reason, in Spain, it gave him a little confidence. I was so proud and watched him the whole time. I did the worst thing a mum can do and cheered when he came back with his drink, but I couldn't help myself. He rolled his eyes so hard I think he could see out of his ears.

Even though he was doing amazing things like this, we still had the problems of being restricted by the routines. Each night we made it out a little longer with them to watch the entertainment. I mean, the kids really could not give a damn about the kids' entertainment; Terry and I enjoyed it so much more than they did. They had a magician and different Disney characters. We were dancing along, singing and were mesmerised by the magician, until the bloody kids ruined it for us and told us we needed to go home as it was getting late. 'Aww, come on, they're just about to do the bubble show, it's not faaaair.' That was me. I said that.

Yes, this really did happen. Sometimes I wonder who the parents are and who the kids are here.

Another issue was the food. We went all-inclusive and thought it was the best idea due to how fussy they are. With all-inclusive they could try as much as they liked, and it didn't matter if they didn't eat it as they could just get something else. That is a great plan as long as the kids like the all-inclusive food. If they don't, you have just wasted a hell lot of money on food they won't eat, which was the case for us. I'm not going to lie; the food was basic, but what could you expect from a 3 star really? They offered chips and nuggets every night for the kids, which sounds great on paper, but Poppy said the nuggets tasted funny (meaning different) and wouldn't eat them and she doesn't like chips. Loves waffles but won't touch chips. She pretty much lived off watermelon and pancakes the whole time we were there, bless her. By the time we got home, she had lost weight, so I don't think we will make that mistake again. I think next time we don't do all-inclusive and pack a hell of a lot more food for her.

The funniest thing I did though was to pack a book in my suitcase. I packed a book to read on the sun lounger. Yep, I don't know what made me completely forget what my kids are like, but it made me laugh when I opened my luggage and found it there. Ah, what expectations I had from this holiday. I think I got to sit and chill out on a sun lounger for about five minutes for the whole time we were there. We were chasing the kids around the water park, making sure Poppy wasn't drowning as she couldn't swim, chasing them to put more sun cream on and making sure Fin hadn't just decided to run off all together. Then they insisted that we kept going on the slides with them and one of the tunnel ones almost knocked me out. I wasn't expecting to suddenly hit speeds of around 90mph and forget how tall I am. My head knocked on the top of it forcing me to lay down, which makes you go bloody faster. I am whizzing round the corners like a rocket that is about to take off, until at the end, you plop out like a massive turd being dunked to the bottom and come out barely able to breath, my eyes stinging from my mascara running down my face, thinking how the fuck is this fun?

In between them needing a wee every half hour, wanting a drink or food, hurting themselves and needing a plaster, you don't get to chill out at all. But like I said, seeing them happy is worth all of that. It is worth it. It is worth it.

If this had been in the busy school holidays, I think it would have been a very different experience. We have always gone away out of the school holidays, so it is quieter for them as our children deserve to enjoy their holidays as much as any child does, which is why I will always argue the school fines for taking kids on holiday. This never bloody happened when we were young; parents could take their kids out when they liked. It is just another way for the government to make some money from us, but the joke of it is, the fine is still less than the price the holiday companies charge during the school holidays! Hardly a deterrent and even then, only for the poor.

Holidays are definitely not for the weak though. If anything, the government should be bloody paying me for giving the teachers a break for a week! For most autistic children, home is their safe place. Stepping away from that is scary. That's why we end up taking a hundred bags with us as we basically have to recreate their safe place in another location. We packed sensory lights, endless toys, books, cuddlies, the white noise machine, some safe food, their quilt covers. I realise this sounds like a round of the generation game.

If you haven't been away with the kids before, I would recommend booking somewhere cheap and close to home, so you can get back easily if it all goes to shit. A hot tub, if possible, always seems to be a winner. The kids love chilling in it, and it gives you a little break from having to keep them happy all the time. (Although you do have to make sure they don't drown too much.) And, of course, the most important thing of all – find somewhere that has WiFi.

Listen, holidays are great if you lower your expectations of how they will be. Kids will not stop moaning and whinging just because they are on holi bobs, and autistic kids will not suddenly stop caring about routine either. I usually find the first night is the worst. The kids are unsettled because it is a new place and very likely to sleep even less than they usually do. As with most things, it takes them time to adjust to their holiday and with mine they will just start fully settling in properly and enjoying it the day before we come home.

Every. Single. Time.

So, in a nutshell, holidays are great and a fantastic experience for the kids but if you are looking for a truly relaxing one, a trip to rejuvenate your mind and replenish your spirit, don't take the kids with you.

Top Tips

☆ *Use social stories to prepare your child for holiday and find pictures of where you are going.*

☆ *Lower your expectations and remember that they will most likely have a breakdown because of the change of routine.*

☆ *Try to set up their bedroom as the same layout at home. That is, if the wall is on their right side of their bed at home, make sure that is the same there. Take quilt covers to keep that the same.*

☆ *Take as much safe food with you as you can possibly pack.*

☆ *Use sunflower lanyards at the airport and ask for special assistance.*

Chapter Twelve

BENEFITS BRITAIN

This is quite the controversial subject, but I am going to write about it as I think there needs to stop being such a stigma around this. Yes, benefits. This is something that is known to make a lot of people angry, so let's discuss it.

We might as well start with work, as this is where the problems begin. Before I had Fin, I was working for a company that signed people up to do NVQs in the workplace. This is over 11 years ago, so I have no clue if they are even called NVQs anymore – if they are not, they are qualifications for anyone who doesn't know. This involved lots of driving, all over the place to different workplaces. It was not fun being heavily pregnant, I can tell you that. I think I would have preferred a physical job, because sitting in the car for hours is unbelievably uncomfortable when you have a 7lb baby sitting on your bladder. Anyway, after maternity leave, I actually couldn't go back as Terry had taken my job. He was made redundant from his old job a week before I was due to give birth, so we needed a quick replacement, which was my position. I can't even begin to tell you the stress this caused but thankfully, with my position waiting for him at work it was OK, but it did mean I had to leave during maternity.

After having Fin, I tried to find anything that would

bring in some money while looking after a baby. So I tried a bit of Avon, and Betterware, and soon realised it wasn't worth it for me. I was bringing home hardly any money at all but walking all day long. Great for me exercising but that was about it. I then got a job at Tesco. It was night work as this was all I could do. Terry was working in the day, so couldn't have Fin and there was no one else. The shifts I did were 8pm until 2am. This doesn't sound too bad but honestly it was the worst. For one thing, Fin was awake at around 5am every morning, which left hardly any time for me to catch up on sleep. I missed the evenings with Terry. The only time we had child free was our evenings and now that was gone, and every parent knows, the best part of the day is when the kids are asleep in bed, and you can catch up on your TV time. And you know the worst thing? They stuck me in the bloody freezers. As if I wasn't suffering enough, I now had to freeze to death while there. It was awful and I hated every second of it.

I worked there right up until Poppy was due as I wanted as much maternity as possible for after. But while I was off, I found another position at a call centre for emergency lifelines. It was actually a really great job, mostly speaking to elderly people and trying to get help for them. Many of them had dementia and would sometimes call up about the strangest things. One person was sure the army soldiers were in her house. She wasn't frightened by them, she just found them rude as she kept offering them a cup of tea, but they were ignoring her.

The best thing to do with dementia patients is to go along with what they are saying, as it will only scare them to tell them that no one is there. So, I would quite enjoy getting her to put me on the phone to these imaginary soldiers and having a go at them for being so bloody rude! It prepared me for living with Poppy and all the imaginary conversations I must have with SpongeBob constantly.

The other good thing about this position was the fact it was flexible working again and in the evenings. Though starting and finishing earlier, around 5.30pm to 10.30pm, it was tough as some of the start times were 5pm. This would put a hell of a lot of pressure on Terry to get home in time so he would often work through his lunch. He would sometimes be late, and I would have to make up the time, or sometimes he would get back at literally 5 minutes to 5 and I would have to dash there as quick as I could, without even a chance to say hello to him.

Once again, our evenings were lost, and even worse this time as we literally would high five each other at the door and then go. We barely saw each other. But I carried on bringing in the money. It was the only job that worked around the kids. I had no one they could go to, no childcare, no after school clubs – it's different when you have children with additional needs. Being brutally honest, there is nothing for them and no one wants to look after them. I worked at the office all through lockdown as it was classed as an essential service. It was only when lockdown was over that I broke my foot and couldn't get in.

You couldn't make it up. We had finally been able to come out of our homes and go out and see people, we were leaving the darkness, emerging blinking into the light, reaching to grasp a new future . . .

And then I broke my foot and couldn't leave the house again.

I remember it so clearly as I was carrying Poppy down the stairs. My footing went but I kept holding her. In order to not drop her, I held her tight, but all my weight went on to my foot, it went from beneath me and bent the wrong way. I was at the bottom of the stairs screaming in agony, watching my ankle swell up before my eyes. I was sobbing as Terry helped walk me into the lounge. He had been in the shower and rushed out as quick as he could. We came into the lounge to find Fin still sitting there on his tablet. He barely looked up. 'Fin,' I said. 'Could you not hear me screaming? Why didn't you come and help?'

'I was trying to finish my game!' he replied and that was that. Oh, I'm sorry that I may have disturbed your very important game by falling down the stairs and nearly breaking my neck. I will be more quiet next time!

During this time of being stuck at home with a broken foot, I started Instagram and TikTok. I was sitting around a lot, so I started to post about everyday life and autism, and I suddenly realised there were a lot of people out there, in a similar position to me. My account started to grow quite quickly, and I was in shock. For the first time in my life, people actually wanted to listen to me.

I shared more and more about my life bringing up autistic children and I did it with comedy a lot of the time. I found a lot of autism pages could be quite serious and I wanted something that was a bit more light-hearted for people, as sometimes we have to laugh at the situations. Sometimes your only options are to laugh or cry. I'd rather laugh.

The more I posted, the more my following grew, and I started getting requests to do adverts and then I realised

I could hopefully do some good with my page, as well as making some money.

I started to get close to some other content creators, and we decided to protest to government for our children's rights in school, we called it SEND Reform England. This came about when a councillor from Kent County Council made some statements such as 'getting an EHCP was the in thing to do'. Obviously, this angered so many people as it fed into what ignorant people believe about us parents, that we simply just want all the benefits that come from raising children with additional needs and it is some kind of trend. The councillor did go on to apologise and resign from his position. However, in my eyes, the damage had been done.

After our big protest with over 1,000 people attending, we ran petitions, spoke to MPs, spoke in parliament, as well as having a parliamentary drop in and went on to run 13 more protests across England. To say it was stressful would be an understatement. We constantly had people telling us we were doing it wrong, or what about their area? They called us clout chasers and were angry when their one email in 350 wasn't replied to. And all the while, we were volunteers not getting a penny for all the work we were doing, as well as working our own jobs and trying to fight for our own children.

But despite all this, it was worth it. This community stood together (literally in the pouring rain sometimes) and put SEND in the mainstream media, like it never had been before and to all the people that supported and continues to support us, I will forever be grateful.

Running SEND Reform England, as well as my social

media pages on TikTok, Instagram and Facebook, became a full-time job. I call it a job as it makes me money, but I really don't see it that way as I do love what I do. A job really only feels worthy of that word if you hate it, but it did start to bring in more money than me actually going out to work did, so I decided to resign from my work at the call centre.

I was on a minimum wage there and me doing one advert for a perfume could bring in more money than me working 20 hours for a company, so it made sense.

I have to tell you though, one of the first adverts I did was for a dildo! Yes, a dildo. I had no idea how I was going to sell this with a straight face, so I ended up filming it as if the dildo was a friend of mine. As I was filming me skipping and dancing with a dildo in my garden, I wondered what my life had become and if social media was actually the route I wanted to go down.

Please don't get excited and think I'm rich through TikTok. Hell no. Far from it. We live in a two-bed house the size of a shed with one toilet. I walk around in mostly Primark clothes, while the kids are in Nike. But it does bring in slightly more than my last job did. Plus, I don't even have to leave my house, so it was a win in my eyes.

The problem is a lot of SEN parents find it impossible to work and are forced to leave their jobs. Most don't want to be on benefits, but it is the only option. To be honest, it's not even just SEN parents, I think all parents have this struggle – it is bloody hard to find a job that fits into school hours and gives you all the holidays off! You could argue the fact that there are holiday clubs and after school clubs the kids can go to, not to mention family taking them but like we have said before, these options aren't there a lot of the time for SEN children. I can't imagine putting them into a club during the holidays – they would literally be beside themselves. The trouble with the in-between children once again is that they have the knowledge and understanding of what is going on. They would know it is the school holidays and they are basically being sent into school again and there is no question that they wouldn't cope with doing an after-school club. They so desperately need to be home after school to chill out. Yes, maybe all children need this, but I feel that autistic children like mine are working doubly hard to get by at school, especially if they are in mainstream. This is draining on them, and by the time the school day is done, so are they. Taking them to a group afterwards would just lead to more meltdowns.

Therefore, we have the first issue with finding a job. It needs to be basically in between the hours of 9.30am and 2.00pm and during term time only. Mmmm ... A dinner lady maybe? Lollypop man? The options are very limited. If you miraculously manage to find a position within these times, you then need to consider all the phone calls you will get from the school and all the medical appointments you need to attend. Your employer must be OK with you being on call 24/7 and possibly having to suddenly leave at any moment.

So, as you can see, it's not that easy to just get a job. People also forget that being a full-time carer, who is up several times during the night, is extremely tiring too. Can you really expect carers to care full time for no money as well as try to bring in a wage? It is impossible and would run people into the ground. Not to mention how dangerous it can be trying to live on little to no sleep and possibly having to commute to work.

On top of being unemployed, you then have all the extra costs that come with raising disabled children. Larger nappies for children and adults, sensory equipment and fidget toys, seam free clothing, extra-large buggies and wheelchairs, bed safety tents, waterproof mattresses, safety car seats, ear defenders, white noise machines, tablets that get broken a lot and need replacing, commodes, the list goes on and on . . . and then you have the activities that you need to pay extra for. For example, mine could not attend normal swimming lessons as they wouldn't be able to pay attention to the instructions when speaking to a large class, so we have to pay for SEN swimming lessons. These are smaller groups, so they always cost more money. They also did horse riding at a disabled riding centre. Once again, this costs more money but was also needed as therapy sessions for them. The bike riding lessons we paid for were one-to-one lessons. They were incredible and really helped them to learn but if we didn't have financial support, there would be no way we could have ever afforded this, and our children would have never learned to ride a bike or swim.

This is why benefits are so important. This gives our disabled children the things they need, and that money is for them. Not us. As much as the media tries to make people believe that everyone claiming it are just sponging off the system and can't be bothered to go out to work, in reality the carers in this country are saving the taxpayers millions by looking after the most vulnerable for zero pay. I personally believe the real crooks are the ones in charge who made the decisions that led to the poorest being worse off, while some huge companies continue to avoid paying fair taxes. They're the challenge, not Chloe, the single mum working a part-time job while, trying to look after her autistic child, claiming just enough benefits to not die.

You often hear people saying things like 'you shouldn't be paid for looking after your own child!' Well, one, that goes for most people in the UK then as most people are entitled to child benefit. I wonder if the person moaning about people not getting paid for their own children has refused their child benefit payment? I imagine probably not. And two, it becomes care duties when parents are doing more than the average parent would be expected to. Yes, every parent should expect to change nappies for the first few years, they wouldn't be expecting to do this with a 15-year-old that is now bigger than them and more aggressive. This is no longer simple parenting; this is full-time caring for someone.

Obviously, this is just an example out of millions of different scenarios, but we would be here forever if I were to list them all. My children are not classed as high-care needs, but I still have to do care duties that go above and beyond the norm at the age they are. I still have to hold their hand when crossing the road as they can't be trusted when they become distracted. I still have to feed Poppy and cut up her food for her and she will need constant encouragement to eat. I still get up several times throughout the night with them, much like the newborn days. I still have to do personal care, which I won't go into due to their privacy. The list goes on … so you can only imagine how much attention a high-care-needs child needs if my low-care-needs children still require this.

People's ignorance astonishes me, and their anger towards parents for claiming benefits that they've picked up from some biased tabloid.

I find it quite ugly to be honest, and almost like they are jealous that someone is getting something they are not. I am sure most parents would happily choose their children to have no care requirements instead of receiving a payment every month. Let's be real here too – the payments are so minimal they don't even cover the amount of baby wipes I get through in a day.

I wish this stigma would go, but unfortunately there are always the minority that are taking the piss and claiming when they shouldn't, that ruins it for everyone. They are the ones that make it so difficult to receive any payments in the first place, and they are the ones that cause people like my dad, with Parkinson's disease and dementia, to still have to prove their disability every year. Funnily enough, the Parkinson's hasn't just gone away, no. Still disabled!

I do wonder though if people really do make it up. I mean, filling out 100 pages about your child's needs is such hard work! How many times have you put off filling out the DLA forms? The dreaded forms that fill me with horror when they come through. Would people really go through all of that just to make up their medical needs? I guess the paperwork is made like that as a deterrent. You have to really want it to be filling it all out, and the questions are so ridiculous. They might as well put things like 'Can they breathe unsupported?' Yes, of course they can! And the results will then be, no help required. Great!

I don't really know why I am writing about this because I am assuming you are already a SEN parent to have even bought this book and you already know how bloody expensive our little people are. I hope though, that for someone who has been too ashamed to apply for these benefits, they may realise that there is nothing to be ashamed of and it is something that is vital for your child.

Or, if you already have this benefit, you can just ignore this whole section or maybe you can tear these pages out and post them to an ignorant twat that you know. Another option could be just using them as your toilet paper – I wouldn't judge you; we need to save money after all as the benefits are shit.

Top Tips

☆ *You do not need a diagnosis in order to claim DLA.*

☆ *Don't be ashamed or feel guilty for claiming benefits for your child. This is money they are entitled to to help support them in life.*

☆ *If you are on a low income, you can also apply for carers allowance on top of the DLA.*

☆ *If your child receives high-rate mobility, you may be able to apply for a car. However, please remember the car will be used to replace the DLA benefit. You won't receive both.*

Chapter Thirteen

THE SEN-BETWEENERS

I am surprised it has taken me this long to get to this chapter, as really this was the whole reason for me writing the book. I wanted to talk about the in-between children in more detail, or the ghost children some call them.

Having kids that are kind of in-between is really tough at times, as you feel like you don't fit anywhere. Half the people think your child is behaving odd or just badly behaved, the other half think you are a fraud and there is nothing wrong, or not wrong enough. It is hard to find a group that gets it. The mainstream school parents don't understand what a struggle everything is and find it odd that my child is behaving in certain ways, but then the parents of high-care-needs children are wondering what on earth I am complaining about, as it can't be hard work surely when they can talk and take themselves to the toilet, etc.

You feel like you want to walk around with a T-shirt on saying, 'He is autistic even though you wouldn't know.' I guess that is what the sunflower lanyard is for, but the ironic thing is, he can't wear it because of the sensory issues he has being autistic.

I can't tell you the number of times I have been at a park and spotted another autistic child, I say it with confidence as I think when you know you know. Wearing ear defenders, stimming . . . all the signs. Whereas my child isn't displaying those obvious signs, so the other parent will never know my child is autistic too. I want to tell the other parent so badly, but I realise I may come off a little strong. So, I try to sneak it into the conversation. I start telling them really random things about how he doesn't like loud noises and may not talk to her child. She's probably thinking, 'OK, I didn't even ask.' But this is what happens when you get so desperate for a place to fit into. You try to find the people that will understand.

Making friendships are not easy though and it is especially hard finding a support network. At times it can feel like a competition between parents, which is something I find quite off putting. I always assumed the competition would be over things like winning races, getting into the best schools and how many A's they get but never who has the most disabilities.

What a weird competition to be in – who is the winner here? It really can be the strangest conversation. 'My child was diagnosed with autism.' 'Mine was diagnosed with autism and global delay.' 'Mine was diagnosed at age one because they are so severe.' 'Well, mine was diagnosed while in the womb!' Honestly, it would not surprise me if certain people said this.

It is like I have said before, who decides who is severe and who isn't? I can appreciate there are low and high-care needs with autism and there can be a huge difference between these children. I can only imagine how incredibly hard it must be to raise a child with no communication, and I am so grateful that my children can express if they are hurt or upset.

However, some people will say my children must have

autism mildly. I think they say this because they are looking at my child speaking, they are seeing them display many signs of a neurotypical person, mainly because of masking. But when I watch my child mid meltdown, screaming and hurting themselves, missing out on events because they just can't cope, I find the word 'mild' a bit of a kick in the teeth to be honest.

There is nothing mild about their feelings and emotions, there is nothing mild about your child saying they don't wish to be here anymore.

I saw a quote once that said, 'I don't have mild autism, you are just experiencing my autism mildly.' I thought it was perfect and so true, especially for our maskers. Like the swan you see swimming along slowly and gracefully but below the water, their feet are going crazy.

The trouble is with being the in-between child, people expect more from you. They can't understand why your child can't go to the party. Well-meaning people will say that they will be fine and to bring them along anyway. There won't be many people there and we will keep the music low. They can hang out with your child and so on . . . Until you get there, and your friend has completely forgotten everything she promised. The place is filled with people, lights flashing and music blaring. She spots you and screeches in your child's ear while hugging them, something you know your child hates. She tells your child they can go upstairs and play with her child, but you know this is the last thing your kid wants to do. You last there as long as you possibly can before you can see your child is getting worked up. You say you need to go, and you know that secretly she is thinking you worry too much. She tells you once again how 'fine' your child is, when you know they are anything but fine. But how would they know, I guess? They don't see the aftermath. They see your child silent but appearing OK. They don't realise that child is going to break down at home, sob uncontrollably for a few hours and be too overwhelmed to sleep. We are the ones who have to deal with the fallout from the events.

The children that stay silent are usually the ones who are forgotten about in class. If they are not disruptive, they are sadly left. Unseen for better or worse, and this is why they are stuck in limbo too often. They are not severe enough for SEN school but can't cope with mainstream.

I always tell people that Fin wouldn't fit into a SEN school as much as he doesn't fit into mainstream. A SEN school wouldn't stimulate him enough academically and I think he would find it quite chaotic. I look at children like Poppy, who would be classed as a wild child. Feral at times even. She likes to run, slam doors, vocal stim loudly, flood the toilets and throw things, whereas Fin needs order and structure. He needs a quiet space to learn. But mainstream doesn't offer this either. In classes of 30–38 kids, it will always be noisy. He needs extra attention from the teachers to help with his everyday tasks. So, where the hell do these kids go that don't fit the mould but have so much potential?

That is why we were beyond happy to find Fin's secondary school, a school for the in-between children. It seemed too good to be true, like a dream school for the kids who don't fit anywhere else. This school is only offered to children with an autism diagnosis and an EHCP. The children who attend cannot have any behavioural issues and need to be at a certain standard academically. This seemed to match Fin perfectly, so I booked an appointment to look around it.

When I went to see it, I burst into tears when leaving. It was the most perfect school I have ever seen, and I didn't even know these types of schools existed. I cried from the fear that he may not get accepted there, and also for the thousands of children that will never go to a place like this, knowing it could change their lives.

I walked through the doors and was met straight away by the school dog and walked through to the open meeting area. The classes are a maximum of 13 students and every class has a quiet room attached to it. The quiet space has fidget toys in it but without a door to separate; so, the child could sit in there in a calmer environment, but also listen to the teacher talking so they can continue to learn.

We were taken around the school further and found it had a farm onsite. Yes, an actual farm with chickens, pigs and sheep in the most beautiful setting. Once a week they go to muck them out, pick the eggs and care for them.

We then went on to the playgrounds and found outdoor and indoor trampolines, outdoor gyms and rooms with Nintendo Switches in. Fin was totally sold when he saw this, of course, and I am now a little concerned that he thinks he is just going to be playing games all the time at secondary school.

As we wandered down the halls, I could see lots of posters about autism. Something that I found strange as I assumed they wouldn't actually talk about being autistic there. I was so happy to find that they are very open about their autism and have meetings to talk about their struggles with autism, but also their achievements. What a great way to make children never be ashamed of being autistic.

I went on to find the toilets, which were individual ones with an individual sink in them. Some were without hand dryers and some with. A picture was on the door to show which ones had them so the children could avoid those ones if they didn't like the noise.

Even the colour scheme of the school was decided by autistic people and was found that these were the most calming of colours. Absolutely everything had been thought of here.

I honestly think I walked around with my mouth gaping open the whole time. It felt like being in Willy Wonka's Chocolate Factory. It is a school built for neurodivergent children and I have not ever in my life entered a single place that is like this. After our kids have spent their whole life in this neurotypical world not built for them, it was like my heart sighed walking through those doors as it was finally somewhere they belong.

A sense of belonging is something that is so often missing from a life with autism, and a lot of our children know it too. They know they don't quite fit, and I think that is why they gravitate to other autistic people somehow. Honestly, both children rarely speak to other kids but when we are at a park if they start talking to another child, it is almost always because they are neurodivergent too.

Even as I felt overjoyed for Fin to find a school like this for him, I then wondered if this would ever be a place that Poppy could possibly go to. Would Poppy be classed as an in-between child at all. She is at a SEN school and her teachers even struggle with her there. She doesn't sit and learn very well at all and can be very disruptive, but having said that, she is also verbal, and her communication is getting better. She can read and write (when she wants to), so she could have the potential of going to somewhere like this but because of her behavioural issues, she probably wouldn't be accepted, so once again, my child is stuck in limbo. Where does she fit in this grand scale of severe and mild autism, the in-between ones, the delayed ones, the ones with behaviour problems and the masking ones. I think she is a little bit of all of them to be honest.

The local authorities and government love to go on about being more 'inclusive' in mainstream school, without actually understanding what that looks like. Putting all children into the same bracket and teaching them all exactly the same is not being inclusive. Take this hypothetical situation, for example, five children are given access to a playground. They all have the same rights as each other. They all get to go in this playground for an hour, they are free to choose what they like in this playground. There is no special treatment here and all are treated the same. But one of the children is in a wheelchair and the park is only accessible with a ramp, which it doesn't have. The person in charge says that if they add an entrance with a ramp for that child then this would not be fair to the others as they all need to be treated the same. This is the local authority's idea of being 'inclusive'. That is not being inclusive at all, as this is actually excluding the child in the wheelchair from being able to use it.

An expression I recently heard broke my heart. The

person told me that the children with additional needs stuck at mainstream school are now being referred to as 'corridor children'. This is because many of them are unable to cope with the classrooms, so they are separated and stuck at a desk outside of the classroom on their own. Is this really what inclusion looks like? If it is, I don't want it.

I find that Fin worries so much about everything and his anxiety can hold him back. I often say he has the weight of the world on his shoulders. He is very much a 'glass half-empty' kind of guy. Even when they were teaching about global warming at school and the teacher was saying about how cars are bad for the planet, he then didn't want to get in the car. It took ages for me to persuade him to get in. Once we were sat in the car, he would shout at me to hurry so we could leave immediately, so we weren't spending any time leaving the engine running. I look at Poppy and know she doesn't carry the weight of the world on her shoulders like Fin does. She still gets upset and gets scared by things, but she lets those emotions out. But with Fin, it is like he is keeping them all in until they explode. And I think it is because of the awareness that he has that Poppy lacks. Too aware in fact, where he thinks people are laughing at him when they are not.

It is very tricky, as obviously, it is harder for autistic people to read people's faces so sometimes Fin doesn't pick up social cues. Actually, he never picks up on social cues and this means he can take offense quite a lot when no one was being mean. Even just simply chuckling because he said something cute can lead to him getting really upset, so we have to be really careful to not embarrass him. It's rich though seeing as he embarrasses me literally all the time and will tell people my most private details. Talking of privates . . . this has reminded me of when Fin was younger and misunderstood things.

Their topic at school was on Africa and I explained to Fin that me and Terry had gone to Kenya on Safari for our honeymoon and asked if he wanted to take some photos in to show them. He wanted to take the whole album in, but I explained to him the rest of the pictures were private so he could only take a few. The pictures were just of us drinking and going out to eat (nothing dodgy, I promise), but still there wasn't really any need to show them to the kids and teachers. The teacher came and spoke to me as I went to pick him up that evening, she had quite the smirk on her face when she told me that Fin had said, 'These are all the photos I can show you, as the other ones are of mummy and daddy's privates!' I wanted the ground to swallow me whole. I was laughing while explaining that I just said they were private, not meaning private parts. However, I could also feel myself going red. Seriously, why do our bodies betray us like this? It was making me look so guilty, she probably still doesn't believe me to this day!

As much as my kids struggle with interpreting the world around them, they also have the most incredible way of looking at things. These children were born to think outside the box, and I think the in-between kids, like Fin, may be incredible in the workplace when they are older, if given the opportunity.

There are moments that catch me off guard. I am still amazed by them every day, with their way of looking at the world or their way of thinking. One year, we were bringing the Christmas tree down and I started to decorate it. By the way, I did try to get the kids involved, but what they do is clump a load of baubles together at the bottom to make it look really shit and then bugger off and go back on their tablets. Anyway, I was in the middle of decorating it and Fin began to get really upset. He told me that the baubles were in the wrong place.

Now, we don't have simple red and green baubles, we have crazy ones that are a complete mismatch. We have some reindeer ones, snowmen, holly, bells, personalised ones, Santa and even the *Nightmare Before Christmas* ones. He started to point out where each one needed to be and moved some that I had put in the wrong place. I thought there was no possible way that he would remember where they were before, but I decided to check back through pictures on my phone of last Christmas as he was so adamant, and I couldn't believe it. He was spot on. He was placing the baubles in the exact place they had been in the previous year. Maybe I was wrong all along . . . maybe he is *Rain Man*, and I should be booking a trip to Las Vegas immediately.

Poppy will often surprise us too; she will seem like she is off in Poppy land and completely unreachable. She will be talking to her invisible friends and dancing around the place and suddenly will ask a question relating to what I was just talking about. I was in the other room speaking with friends on the phone (I thought, quite quietly) without realising she was actually listening to the conversation. How she does this while talking and playing I will never know, but it has taught me to be careful around her, as I never know what she is going to repeat and to who.

Another reason to watch what we say is because of them being literal thinkers too. Sarcasm is something that confused them for a long time; Fin seems to get it a bit now but Poppy it still confuses.

The literal thinking can be funny though. I have entered the kitchen seeing a plate just thrown on the floor and wondering why. I went back to Fin and looking shocked, he explained that I told him to chuck it in the kitchen, so that is exactly what he did. It is usually more subtle than this though and I get glimpses of how their mind works. Even with me simply moaning that the house is a mess. I will march around the room very loudly and angrily picking up their toys and say things like 'Nobody ever helps me around here!' or 'Would be nice if people just picked up their things!', and the kids will just ignore me. Now this may come across as so rude, I'm like erm hello? Get the hint! But they don't. I haven't spoken to them directly or asked them to do it, so why would they assume I am talking to them and my anger is aimed at them. I needed to speak to them directly and say, 'You have created this mess, now please go and pick it all up.' I must point out though that the same thing seems to happen with Terry ignoring me when I do this, however he is definitely just ignoring me on purpose!

This is another reason that I think so many people come out with things such as 'everyone's a little bit autistic' or 'why is there so much autism now? There was none back in my day', but the truth is, it was there but it was not recognised like it is now.

These children would have been the in-between children

at school, they would have been the ones classed as 'weird' or 'naughty'. I remember several children in my class at school that no one spoke to. I am pretty sure these children were neurodivergent, and it makes me sad to think of how hard their lives would have been for them at mainstream. Neurodivergent people are not spreading, it's not contagious. Luckily, the doctors and scientists have researched over the years and recognise the traits more now, and that's a good thing. It's not that more people need help, we're just better at spotting people that need help now.

Obviously, the sad thing is, the children that were classed as having severe or complex needs were hidden away in institutes, so you also didn't see them, and this is why people are so misinformed when thinking there is some kind of autism pandemic spreading across the world. Autistic people have always been there – you just didn't notice them.

Again, another damaging comment is 'everyone is a bit autistic'. Not everyone is autistic though and people need to stop saying this . . . No one can be a little autistic; you are either autistic or you are not. Again, this is describing the in-between children and basically saying they are a little bit autistic, which is just not the case – you actually mean you just see a few of their traits but not all of them.

Many of these incredible children will, unfortunately, be forced into mainstream schools as there are just not enough SEN schools to cater for them due to the lack of funding they receive. Because of this, I believe mainstreams need to be adequate to support SEN children and should all have a learning space that is for children with additional needs and disabilities. If they don't have this, then they are not suitable. I do want to remind you all that you can ask for reasonable adjustments to be made for your child.

Reasonable adjustments don't usually cost the school anything, so don't be afraid to march in there and ask. OK, calm down. You don't need to march in there angrily – only do that if they say no to your requests. Then I'll be right behind you.

Some of the adjustments could be as simple as a flexible school uniform. If they are more comfortable in leggings and a polo top, does it really matter? Just let them do it. Regular breaks are a must! Avoiding the crowds by coming to school slightly later. Fidget toys to help them concentrate.

It saddens me to think of so many of our children being let down. These in-between children could possibly get jobs, live alone or come out of school with qualifications if given the correct support, but they are written off before they have even started by being forced into a one-size-fits-all approach. One size most definitely does not fit all, the world needs to celebrate differences more and the people who think outside the box. These people are the great minds of this world, they are the creators and developers, the ones to push science to its limits and see things in a completely unique way. Without our amazing neurodivergent people, the world would be very boring indeed.

Top Tips

☆ *Ask your child's mainstream school to make reasonable adjustments for them.*

☆ *Don't throw your child in the deep end, take time to let them adjust.*

☆ *Don't allow people to dismiss their feelings.*

☆ *Remember that speech doesn't mean they can communicate easily; offer other alternatives still.*

Chapter Fourteen

P.A.R.T. Why? (Seriously, why are we doing this?)

Events such as Christmas, Halloween and birthdays can always be a little bit stressful to say the least. I think it is easy to see why our kids can sometimes get overwhelmed at these times. Even I do as an adult to be fair.

First of all, there's the build-up, and the shops have a lot to answer for when it comes to this. I've actually found Christmas decorations in Tesco as early as October. Yes, before Halloween. Terry and I have a running joke about the store manager at the Tesco near us - we genuinely believe he hates Halloween. We're not sure what happened to him in his life at Halloween. Maybe he found a carrot in his trick-or-treat bag, maybe experienced a particularly scary trick or encountered an overzealous pumpkin. Who knows? Whatever trauma he's been through, he can't wait for Halloween to be over so he can get on with Christmas.

You get a week, max, to grab your Halloween bits at this store. By the end of the day on the 30th of October, the staff are already hard at work dismantling it all. It's absolute chaos walking into the store. Staff are up on ladders, practically chain sawing the Halloween signs, while others are chucking pumpkins out the doors. Cages are rolled out, half-full of all the decorations that'll be stashed away out back until next year. You enter the store on actual Halloween day, and the store's been stripped bare of anything Halloween – it's already Christmas. You haven't even been bloody trick or treating yet!

So anyway, you can imagine how long this build up to a child is. It would feel like forever before Christmas day was here. Not to mention the bloody elves coming to do their countdown. This will be my biggest advice I can give to you, if you learn nothing else from this book please remember and listen to this: DO NOT START THE ELF ON A SHELF THING. It is a festive ball and chain from which you can never escape. You may think it is some harmless fun in the beginning and may even enjoy the first year of it, but trust me when I say, four years down the line you will suddenly be waking in a cold sweat at 1am realising you haven't moved the fucking thing and having to creep around the house like a bloody burglar, regretting all your life choices.

Once more for the people at the back: DO NOT START THE ELF ON A SHELF THING. You have been warned.

As well as the months of build up to Christmas, there is also the change of how the room looks with all the decorations, which can be quite scary for our kids. Now mine are usually OK with the tree going up, but it is the coming down, that is the problem. They are so distraught each time I so much as take a bauble off, so we have to do it gradually.

Honestly, we start to take one ornament down a day. Bit by bit, a festive death of a thousand cuts. I am surprised we are not still doing this in August with the number of decorations we have.

A couple of years ago, Poppy was so upset to see the

Christmas tree gone that we decided to give her a birthday Christmas tree. Her birthday is in January, so there really wasn't much point in us taking it down and putting it up again, but we actually bought a bigger one. We decorated it with streamers and had balloons blown up small instead of baubles. We hid some of her presents in there and she absolutely loved it ... and then we realised that we would have to go through the heartbreak of the tree coming down again after her birthday, so it wasn't the best idea we had. Instead of one lot of heartbreak, here you go Pops, have two. I did consider just having a tree up as a constant feature in our room throughout the year rather than deal with another meltdown, but it would drive me too mad. Our house is small enough as it is, without having a bloody great tree constantly in it.

I am still unsure what makes them so upset about the tree coming down as they barely look at it all the time it is up. Putting up the tree is not a glorious family bonding time either like they make out in the films. The whole family lovingly passes the decorations to each other, while the person at the end arranges them on the tree, Christmas songs playing in the background while the fire crackles. Ours is more of a separate affair, though it begins with us all together after I have pestered the kids enough to actually get involved, but then they ruin it you see. They recklessly clump all the baubles together at the bottom on one single branch that is clinging on for dear life, so I have to redo it anyway once they are completely bored and have gone back to their games. This usually occurs before jingle bell rock has run its course ...

You then have all the Christmas events. There are

grottos, nativities, Christmas markets and fairs. It is overwhelming for everyone! For some reason we always take
them to a grotto each year; I think because it is the trad-
itional thing to do, but they actually hate meeting Santa. I
mean, he is absolutely terrifying, so I get it.

You are going to meet the old fat guy, that not only
watches you sleep, but as soon as you nod off, he's going
to creep into your house in the middle of the night. He
is a complete stranger, but brings you gifts in exchange
for a drink and some very specific food. No one knows
what happens if you fail to make a satisfactory offering
to this magical fat man (which just means that everyone
who failed to honour the deal isn't around to tell us what
happened). He also keeps a list of all the children, and for
some he will pass his esoteric judgement and deem them
good, keeping a list of those he deems . . . naughty, what
happens to them we may never know.

He sounds a lot like the local authorities to be honest,
keeping lists of naughty kids.

Anyway, Santa is terrifying.

We have had quite a few grotto pictures of Poppy
clung to Terry crying because she didn't want to be there.
We had found one that was perfect for us but has sadly
closed now. They would open up the grotto trail after
Christmas and you could give a donation to charity, there
would be no Father Christmas at the end which was perfect but they could still walk along the trail and the best
bit was they could take as long as they wished just wandering around the magical pathway as there were no queues!

The school nativities I will miss so much once Fin goes
to secondary school. I am always the pathetic parent

sobbing in the audience so proud of my kids, no matter the part. And I don't think you can get funnier than the part of a flashback. Yes, that is what Fin was. I didn't even know that nativities required this and I can't for the life of me remember what they were flashing back to now, but I do remember Fin running back and forth across the stage to resemble . . . well, the 'flash' before a flashback. I can't laugh though; I was the weather in mine. I was lightning. Apparently, it was bad weather the night Jesus was born. Who knew?

Poppy was an angel in hers, the most beautiful rebellious angel I have ever seen. She threw off her halo several times, as to be expected and I think she may have even stomped on it at some point too. She didn't really join in with the singing or dancing, but she was there spinning in circles at one point and, most importantly, smiling at me throughout the whole thing.

We have tried some of the school fairs, but to be honest they are just too much for the kids. Everything is very different than how their school usually looks and there are way too many people crammed into a small space. Fin once said to me he didn't want to go as all it is, is people standing at tables selling their old rubbish to you and I have to say, I kind of agree, so we don't do that anymore.

So, after you have all these events, days out and school activities, finally the big day is here. And so are the meltdowns. Our new tradition has become a meltdown on Christmas day from the kids and sometimes me. It isn't really a tradition that we like but still, it's a tradition. Christmas day is just too much, filled with stockings from Satan – sorry – Santa, presents from us, and then grandparents' gifts. There is a lot going on at once. As a result, the last few years we have stayed at home just to keep it calmer for them. Poppy, instead of meltdowns, has shutdowns. She seems to completely switch off from us all and goes into herself. She is stuck on her one present that she has managed to open but can't process anything else past it, so it is important for us, and especially for her, that we calm everything down and try our best to not make a huge deal out of Christmas day. Poppy's Christmas dinner is of course nuggets still, but with a side of Yorkshire puddings. Still beige but fancy beige.

So, Christmas can have its ups and downs, the same as Halloween. For many years, Fin actually preferred Halloween to Christmas and it became his special interest. We loved this and could fully embrace everything Halloween. Fin even has decorations up throughout the year, as well as his June birthday party being a Halloween one. This was until Poppy came along and we made the mistake of taking her to a Halloween event in a cave. Saying this out loud now, I realise what a stupid idea this was. Taking a kid who is terrified of the dark to a cave at Halloween is definitely on my list of things NOT to do as a parent. Though I haven't even told you the full story, so don't judge me just yet. Before we did this, we took her on a little ghost train – we thought it was for children and would be fun. The man on the door specifically said, 'Yeah, she'll be fine.' We didn't realise this ghost train was from something out of your nightmares. It had Freddie Krueger jumping out at you, as well as IT, zombies lurking around the corners, the Texas chainsaw guy chasing you and Reagan from the exorcist racing out to grab you . . . the whole nine yards. I nearly pissed myself.

OK, I give you permission to judge me now. I am pretty

sure this has scarred Poppy for life, and she gets quite freaked out with Halloween now. We have to be careful with the places we take her to so that they only have fun, cute Halloween things – not the characters out of all the 18+ horror films.

Look, it was an honest mistake.

Every year we do trick or treating, and it did take Poppy a long time to get to grips with the idea of us knocking on people's doors, but not actually going in. Every house we went to, we had to hold her back as she just started wandering into their home. Then she would try to take all the sweets, so it was us continually shouting 'just one!' at every door we came to. I remember her face looking at us like, 'What the fuck are we doing here then? We are knocking and not going in and then stealing from these people!'

It can be hard to juggle. One child hating Halloween and the other had it as a special interest. Thankfully, the Easter Bunny hasn't caused us any trouble yet, unless it is someone in fancy dress. This can sometimes freak them out.

We once took them to Peppa Pig World; Poppy loved Peppa at the time, so we thought she would love it there. She did love it until we went to the show. When the character turned up, she screamed the place down with fear. I think it is an uncanny valley situation, the character is never going to look in real life exactly as they do on the TV. Especially as you wouldn't really expect Peppa Pig to be 6ft tall; this would freak out anyone! Fin was the one that made me really think about how the kids expected things to look compared to how they actually do. Every time we would arrange a trip somewhere, I would show them promo videos of places we were going to in order for them to feel prepared for what it would look like and what would be there.

He told me this didn't help him and made him more anxious when there as it would always look different and worse than the video. This was so obvious to me after he told me. A promotion video is essentially an advert; of course, it would look different. They always film it on a sunny day, all the staff smiling and welcoming, the food looks great and a close up of all the animals you will get to see. When you turn up though, it's pissing down with rain, the staff are fucking miserable, you get served a bowl of wet chips that you paid £20 for and the only animal you saw all day was a bloody meerkat, because all the others were hiding. I totally get why this would be disappointing, fuck me – I am disappointed too and wished I hadn't seen the video that lied to us.

Days out not living up to expectations is one of the reasons that we don't take Fin out on his actual birthday, and the fact that his happiest place in the world is at home seeing absolutely no one. I mentioned before how we had learned our mistake from parties, so we now spread out their birthdays as they both can get very overwhelmed. Still opposites once again though – Poppy will take her time with her presents. She will open one and then she is stuck on that one, for sometimes the whole day. We can't get her to move on and open anymore. It is lovely that she is appreciating and taking her time with it, but troublesome when family and friends come over to give her theirs and she won't even look at them. Fin, on the other hand, rushes through them like they are going to explode if he doesn't get to them quick enough, so he ends up looking ungrateful and rude. There is no happy medium with these kids, no middle ground.

The worst thing with the present opening though is the fact that the kids have no filter. If you have got them something they don't like or already have, they are as sure as hell going to tell you.

In fairness, Fin has got a little better with this after extensive coaching and tries his hardest to not let his unimpressed face show. He fails, but at least he tries now. There was a time when, well, the less said about Christmas 2018 the better. Him trying to hide how he really feels always comes off as the fake 'cheese' smile he gives for pictures. We call it his Chandler (from *Friends*) smile as there really is nothing natural about it. Because of all of this, present opening fills me with anxiety and I usually ask people to leave their gift and get the fuck out. Well, more politely than that. Sometimes. I just can't stand looking at their hopeful faces waiting for a hug or a scream of joy when that just isn't going to happen.

People find it so hard to accept that you have to do traditions differently for our kids at times. Singing 'Happy Birthday' can be a massive trigger and for the first few years of birthdays, Poppy would cry every time we sang it. It is amazing when people do start to adapt their ways to make life a little better for everyone. My mum started putting all of Poppy's presents unwrapped in a box for her to open. It took the pressure off her and she could actually enjoy looking through her new toys. It's a better way of doing things anyway in my opinion, as you don't have to spend hours wrapping!

Like I said previously, we have stopped doing parties now as it is just something that isn't going to make my kids happy on their birthdays. It took a long time to realise I wanted them to have parties, they did not.

One party we did for Fin was, actually, a huge success. He really enjoyed it, but it was a different day to his actual birthday, so he wasn't too overwhelmed. We decided to hold a party in the woods. There were some woods close by that we knew had a little park area in it, so we set up a party in there. We hung birthday bunting on the trees, we laid out picnic blankets and buckets of toys for the kids. Party food was laid out across the picnic tables and as luck would have it, there was an event on at the field next to it, so the kids could run to get ice cream or go on the bouncy castles (bonus as we didn't have to pay for it).

So not all birthdays have been a disaster, but the one Fin had last year was probably the worst one ever. We made the mistake of booking a holiday the week of his birthday and we were actually travelling home on his birthday. This should have been a three- to four-hour trip but it took seven hours because of all the traffic from Glastonbury. Poor Fin was so upset, we had tried to make his birthday the day before by giving his presents and balloons and the cake to him that day but obviously he is autistic, and the date of his birthday cannot really be changed – it's unacceptable in his eyes, so we had, therefore, completely ruined his birthday.

We have been the lucky ones though with the fact the kids do join in with most celebrations, but just in their own way. I have friends who are not able to put up any decorations, they can't go trick or treating and they can't see family at Christmas. I know they feel a sadness about this. Again, it comes down to the expectations you have as a parent but also everything that is put in your face about the perfect family. But I say to my friends, make your own traditions, and do what you can to keep ones you had before, even if it is without the kids. If they are at school, head to the shopping centres to see the Christmas lights, meet friends for a festive drink or put on a Christmas film in the evenings when (sorry, if) they are asleep. If they can't cope with a Christmas tree up in the lounge, put one up in your bedroom. But also remember, they may not like the decorations now, but it doesn't mean they won't forever.

A tradition isn't what we have read about in books or seen in films, it is simply a way of bonding and making memories, and sometimes we need to be flexible with those traditions. Creating new traditions or adapting old ones isn't a bad thing. As long as our children are happy, it really doesn't matter how our Christmas or birthdays look. Remember you can still embrace the new while missing the old.

Top Tips

☆ *Try to keep big events as calm as possible.*

☆ *Don't feel forced into doing the expected activities such as trick or treating. Take them to places like soft play on those days and they will be emptier.*

☆ *Make your own traditions.*

☆ *Bit of a specific one here but don't take your child to a cave at Halloween time if they are scared of the dark.*

Chapter Fifteen

TO EAT OR ADMIT DEFEAT

I have spoken briefly throughout the book about the kids' eating habits, especially Poppy's. The fact she was terrible with food from birth, so I thought I would go into more detail on this one, as eating was something that gave me the biggest anxiety for a long time with Poppy.

Obviously, you need food to live, but a lot of autistic children don't seem to get that. They seem to think that we are trying to poison them all the time. I am not even talking about vegetables here either. I'm talking chips, pizzas, burger – it's not just the healthy stuff. And I would say this is where there becomes a difference between simply a fussy eater (which many kids are) and an autistic selective eater with sensory issues.

So, you end up having safe foods and unsafe foods.

SAFE FOODS
Nuggets
Waffles
Some dry cereal
Crisps
Chocolate
Yorkshire puddings
Nutella
Kiwi (surprisingly)

UNSAFE FOODS
Everything else!

Over the years we have managed to add to the list of safe foods but usually when we add one, others move into the unsafe section.

I find this part of her autism really hard to relate to, as food is life! I love my food so much, but this wasn't always the case when I was growing up. So, this does give a little faith that she may not be this picky forever. I wouldn't actually mind being a little fussier with my food now, as I might actually lose some weight which would be nice.

We have tried many things to make food more fun. We got little trays that you put the food into sections of. It is almost like a board game and your food follows the trail all the way to the end to get your prize, which is chocolate pudding. Of course, this didn't bloody work as you had to put the pudding at the end, and once she saw the chocolate, there was no hope of her eating anything else. You only follow the trail once before you work out that the chocolate is at the end and just skip straight there.

We also tried sparkly spoons and food decorations. I actually cut the sandwiches into her favourite characters – she then wouldn't eat it as obviously, she doesn't want to eat her friend. Massive fail.

No matter what we tried, we couldn't fool her. She knew exactly what we were up to, and I am sure her PDA plays a part in this also. The more you try to get her to eat, the more she is going to resist.

Another mistake we made was getting a bit cocky. Poppy loved plain pasta, but I really wanted to get a bit of goodness into her, so I added a little cheese and mixed it up. It was honestly the tiniest amount you would ever see but, of course, she knew straight away and immediately spat it out. I then tried to give her the rest of the plain pasta, but she wouldn't touch it. We had lost the safe food! Screw me and my stupid ideas! She really did look at me in that moment like all the trust had gone too, I had betrayed her with cheese.

In the end we just gave in to giving her the beige food options she likes, fed is best! If anyone ever tries to tell you this is not the case, tell them to put their opinions in a little box, and kick it straight up their own arse.

Until you have dealt with a chid rapidly losing weight and possibly being tube fed, you will give them anything to keep them alive. We did also find some vitamins that were flavoured gummies, so they tasted like sweets; luckily, she likes these, so we give them to her every day. A little tip for the ones who won't take them, you can also blend them into their favourite drink and most of the time they won't notice!

Most of the time.

With Fin we have the opposite problem: this kid just doesn't stop eating. We really do need to hire a storage unit for the school holidays to keep all his food in. Day one of the holidays and he has sneaked into the kitchen to get his toast and cereal, then a packet of crisps and a chocolate bar, a Pepperami, snack eggs, a banana, then some more chocolate, a couple of biscuits and some bread sticks, and it's not even 9am. In all seriousness, we do have to control it a little bit. I think some of it is sensory seeking, and some of it is boredom.

Since I don't want him to become one of those people that have to be cut out of their own house, we try to replace a lot with cucumber and carrot sticks, which he actually loves thankfully.

When people blame the parents for a child's fussy eating, I have learned that this is simply not true, especially as I have two autistic children who have both been brought up on the same diet. One barely eats and the other eats practically anything. We don't just feed them a bottle of coke and sneak a McDonald's in the hospital to feed them some nuggets the minute they are born. There is a process that happens before this, which is the child barely eating, so you start to try everything you possibly can. You start with salad but end up at Nutella and bread sticks. It's a natural progression.

We are lucky that Fin loves his food, but he is still very much like Poppy where he will only eat certain brands. (Or off brands.) If they change anything he won't touch it again, and he is way too clever for me to sneak any veg into his food. In fact, I spend a lot of my time picking it out. One of his favourite foods is Birds Eye chicken pies, they are great but have peas and carrots in them. Now Fin does like peas and carrots – just not in anything, so I have to dissect the pie and pick each bit out individually making mealtimes even more fun. I mustn't complain though, at least he does actually eat the veg – it just has to be cooked and served separately.

Beige is the only food allowed on Poppy's plate – actually I tell a lie, there's red for the ketchup. I mean, technically ketchup has tomatoes in it, so really, she is getting some goodness in her from that surely? I sound like

I am joking but these really are the things that go through my mind. For example, Poppy has an iron deficiency. She won't touch meat usually unless it's in a nugget, so even when I order a burger for her, we ask for just the buns. We get some very odd looks at the burger vans, and I wonder if they think we are just cheap as they never charge us for them. When we are at home making them though, we actually wipe the burger over the bun flavouring it with a bit of burger juice. I really don't know why but it makes me feel better, like she is maybe getting a tiny bit of meat in her.

So, I have managed to justify it in my head that she is getting what she needs even though her diet is really restricted. Jam sandwich - strawberries are in jam so therefore she is eating fruit. Yorkshire puddings are made with milk, which has calcium in it. Waffles are made with potatoes, which are a vegetable. Please don't even try to argue with me on any of these, I am not taking questions, and I am not interested in any of your 'facts'.

And how many times have you been told 'Oh, they will eat when they are hungry'?

Actually, Janet, they bloody won't. Do you know what they will do? They will starve. And if they don't starve, they will have a really bad relationship with food throughout their life because they were basically force fed.

I will never understand how adults think it is OK to force feed kids or tell them, 'You eat what I give you.' Can you imagine doing that to a friend? Inviting them round for dinner and find out they are a vegetarian, but you have made steak, so it's tough. Your house, your rules!

I can't stand goat cheese, and I was almost sick when

I ate it by accident once. If someone force fed this to me, I would never trust that person again. Believe it or not, I want my kids to actually like me when they are older, not be fearful of me.

Having said that, I do still feel a fiery rage when my kids tell me they absolutely love the new fish fingers I got them, so I stockpile them in case they run out. I buy every single last one in the shop and fill out the freezer full of them. I make them for the kids the next week, exactly how I made them before, and do you know what they say? They tell me they don't like them anymore. I stare at them in disbelief, convinced once again that my children are trying to annoy me. I then spend the next three months trying to force down fish fingers myself to use them up . . . I had every type of fish finger meal you can think of. A fish finger roast, spaghetti fish fingers, pizza with an extra topping of fish fingers, fish finger sarnie at lunch and fishy fingers and milk for breakfast. OK, maybe I am exaggerating but it felt like it.

I have learned over the years to just be zen and not get so frustrated about it. I know it is easier said than done but stressing over it truly doesn't get you anywhere. I know that they have phases of going off food, not eating much and then growth spurts where they eat more. I have learned some tricks along the way such as giving them frozen peas to eat. They are not keen on cooked ones, but frozen ones taste like little sweets. Chopping up grapes and freezing them works too. Separator plates so you can give a selection of picky bits to your picky eaters.

Getting them to make their own food can really help too, and I am not just being lazy as I have to watch over everything the whole time. Even if it is just some toast, they are far more inclined to eat it if it is something they did themselves.

My biggest tip for getting them to eat is to prepare your own food. Make yourself something really nice that you've been looking forward to, then sit down to enjoy it. Just as you go to take that first bite, watch your kids come over and ask for some – or better yet, lick it right in front of you. This happens every time. Why?

Because you had kids and that is why you can't have nice things.

Top Tips

☆ *Try to not stress if the diet is limited, as long as they are still eating.*

☆ *Try to put a new food on the table with them most nights, even if they won't eat it – encourage them to touch it and smell it.*

☆ *Don't mess with a safe food. Don't add anything to it, leave it in a separate bowl, so they can mix it if they wish to.*

☆ *Speak to the doctor immediately if your child isn't eating and is losing weight.*

Chapter Sixteen

MARRIAGE BC

I believe there are two separate stages of marriage. Marriage BC (not before Christ, but before children) and marriage AC (after children). The two stages are vastly different, but the latter is the one that will really test you.

Terry and I have been together about 16 years. This makes me feel extremely old by the way. We first met at work at a call centre, and he was training me. He had a headset on, and I needed to listen in on his calls, so I asked for him to plug into me. Obviously, Terry was very happy with this and ended up stalking me for the next six months. I say stalking but he was just very overly friendly. OK, that doesn't sound better either - still sounds very creepy. I will try to set the scene. We have a friendly chat and find out we both loved the film *Shaun of the Dead*. It was quite a brief chat, and I didn't think about it again for the rest of the day. The next day I turned up to work and at my desk was the *Shaun of the Dead* DVD. Very sweet, also a little bit creepy. I have to say, it did take me a little while to fancy him. He was hiding behind a big goth flashers jacket, the kind you would see out of the Matrix and slick back hair plastered in hair gel. Believe it or not, this wasn't a hot look.

We became great friends and would spend lunch and breaks together, and I would give him lifts home. He constantly told me we were going to end up together, I would laugh and tell him I only saw him as a friend.

Flash forward three years and we got married. He was right; I think this is the one and only time in his life that I will admit that. We had the most perfect day at Wakehurst Place, a stately home set in the most beautiful gardens. Yes, I know – very posh. We were actually really lucky as it was the first year they were doing weddings, so we got it cheap. I always wonder how our day would have gone if the kids had been here then. It would not have run so smoothly; I know that much. I can just picture me dragging my granny trolley down the aisle full of sensory toys and baby wipes, me chasing Poppy around the field to make sure she didn't dive head first into the giant pond and searching for a quiet room for Fin to go to because of all the meltdowns. Being honest, I am quite glad we could enjoy this day before the kids came along, as much as it seems weird looking at the photos now without them in it. You know when it feels like they have always been here, and I look at the photos and think how did we not even know who they were at that stage?

I think it is important that we got to do some amazing things together before having kids like safari in Kenya, trips to Egypt and Rome. I look back now though and think, God, I didn't appreciate it enough when we were there. It almost seems like a different life, and I can't remember what it was like to just look after me, only getting ourselves ready in the morning. What a dream!

Things like going on safari would just never be possible with our kids, not until they are much older anyway. There was a lot of driving around searching for the animals, and they just don't have that kind of patience. I can just imagine us pulling up in front of a cheetah and Fin breaking the quiet by screaming that there was no WiFi and scaring it off. Not to mention, Poppy would be trying to escape out of the car the whole time as she wants to stroke the 'lovely snuggly lion'.

When the kids came along, it did put a strain on our relationship. I think it probably does for most parents. I never understood why people would say a baby would bring them together more. Sleepless nights and walking around looking like a half dead scarecrow with stains on your top doesn't make your partner want to rip your clothes off. In fact, the only thing you do want to rip off is your partner's fat head because:

1   They are the reason you got into this situation and now have a baby hanging off your boob at every moment.

2   They just really fucking annoy you after having kids – even their breathing seems very loud. And don't even get me started on the sneezes. I really need to get some extra ear defenders for myself just so I don't have to hear the most dramatic, unnecessarily loud sneezes on the planet. I feel like it's attention seeking; there is just no need for it.

Jokes aside, even though it puts pressure on your marriage, I think there is an extra bond that comes with having a child together. Seeing those little people that you both created is just the most beautiful thing and especially if you have a good partner that treats your jobs as equal. I always thought Terry would be a good dad, but I didn't realise how much of a great dad he was until these two little people were here. I remember after giving birth to Poppy, I was being stitched up. The most awful experience I think I have ever had, even worse than the actual giving birth. I was still on the gas and air thankfully, but it wasn't stopping the pain. Laying on the bed with my legs in stirrups still, I searched the room for Terry to hold my hand and then found him holding Poppy in his arms and gazing down at her, with nothing but absolute love in his eyes. I thought 'Great! I've lost him again!' as the kids always come first. But I am glad they do. He is the kind of dad that wants to be at every show they do or meeting with the teachers, he wants to be the one to take them to their swimming lessons and is proud of them no matter what grade they get. He is a dad that wouldn't care if they came to him in ten years to tell him they are gay, he wouldn't care what job they did as long as they were happy.

Many of my friends have guys that seem to think they are the only one doing an actual 'job' and it saddens me that people still think this way. Without making his ego too big, I have been very lucky with Terry. He is a completely hands-on dad and always has been; he's always fed them, changed them and played with them. He has never treated it like he is babysitting my kids; I feel some guys do think that way.

Poor Terry has to put up with a lot though. There have been many times I have called him while he is at work, and I am in a right state. Sobbing down the phone because the babies wouldn't settle, angry that someone at the park had been rude to me or even just me in a panic because I can't find my keys. He is my biggest supporter, but also my best friend. We still laugh and chat like we did when we first got together, and this is something I always advise youngsters – marry your best friend. Looks fade, but your connection and humour won't.

Looking after kids is tough, but it is especially tough when you have no one that can look after the kids because of their needs. I miss our date nights so much, most of the time we are sat in front of the TV in the evenings looking at our phones. Not because we hate each other's company but simply because it is the only time we can fully chill out. The kids are finally asleep, and we can catch up on everything that we haven't been able to in the day. Terry would love for us to use this time in different ways; however, I am too bloody knackered at this point and usually tell him to 'fuck right off with that thing before I cut it off'.

I've always been a bit of a romantic.

We do try to take moments for ourselves, we sneak off and hide in our room to have a cup of tea in the day. It sounds ridiculous but that break is so needed sometimes. I mean, we are always interrupted, that goes without saying. Someone shouts for us, and we both sit in silence, waiting to see who is going to break first. Whoever does is the one to go downstairs and sort out some absolutely bloody silly problem they have, which really didn't need to be sorted out, like there is a fly in the room or this was my all-time favourite one, 'I have one thumb bigger than the other.' Yes, this was Poppy calling for us in despair and as an absolute emergency only for us to explain that she just didn't have her thumbs lined up and they are exactly the same size!

Raising autistic children can definitely put an added strain on your relationship, it can be stressful for everyone. I find that quite often I will take out my stress on poor

Terry because I know I can't with the kids. If the kids have been having meltdowns all day and I haven't managed to get anything done, Terry walks in the house of misery from work with me having a go at him for not putting the bins out last week. It is completely random but because of the stress, I need to let it out somewhere. I often wonder if he actually stops at the pub on the way home and just says he has been stuck in traffic as he is never sure what he is going to get when coming back. When the kids are stressed out and having meltdowns, it has a knock-on effect, and I then start to have a meltdown. I do feel that we approach things like this differently. Terry doesn't seem to get so stressed out when they are upset, he is the calmer one out of us both, whereas I can't relax while they are unhappy. I know I can't be short tempered with the kids because it isn't their fault, but I do need to be snappy at someone – which is of course Terry, so we definitely do fall out sometimes, but it usually doesn't last long.

On days out we will sometimes bicker, especially the actual journey of getting there. How can I put this nicely? Terry and I have different ideas of what makes a good driver. I feel like driving up people's backsides and being bumped around in the jerky car doesn't make a great one. Literally the other day I was trying to drink my water in the car and because he decides to speed off at 100mph it spilt all over me, which he found hilarious. I did not. You may ask why I don't drive? I do actually prefer to do the driving; however, his car has air con and heated seats which mine doesn't, so I am willing to risk my life by getting in his car for the sake of comfort.

And don't even get me started if we get stuck in traffic.

The kids obviously start kicking off and that is when once again, me and Terry turn on each other. We must look like a funny sight to others sitting next to us in the other lanes, two kids in the back screaming the place down, probably hitting each other too and then the two adults in the front shouting at each other and threatening to leave the car and walk.

There is one argument that we have had solidly since the kids have been born and that is days out. Terry would happily stay at home and chill out, whereas I want to get everyone out. Terry likes to be at home as he has been at work all week, whereas I have been at home most of the week, so I want to get out. It is the same argument that I don't think we will ever see eye to eye on. The problem is, I quite often plan out absolutely rubbish days. I make us travel miles and when we get there it is a shit show. Many times, I have thought a trip to the beach would be a great idea, until we are stuck in hurricane force winds, sideways rain and there are no food places or shops open. Terry then stands there with his smug face watching me having a breakdown about another one of my bad choices. So naturally I blame him.

Luckily, that is about the only thing we do row over . . . I think we are just too tired to give a shit really. The thing that works with us is having the same parenting style; we agree on the big things and the things we don't agree on really don't matter, such as what TV show we are going to watch that evening.

Terry does call me too soft at times with the kids, but I think he just doesn't see all the times I have said no. He comes back from work and sees me give in, but actually I have been having battles with them all day and I can't be bothered to have another one now. I really think it does depend on the situation though as I can definitely be the more forceful one with trying to get them to step out of their comfort zone, whereas Terry is happy to just let them be. I guess someone always has to be bad cop.

The thing that really grinds my gears though is they will choose dad over me any day. I am the one that does the majority of stuff for them, school runs, cook their dinner, get them new clothes, take them out but no, Terry is the fun one. He is the one that does pretend fights with them and throws them around the place. I try to be the fun one too, but I feel like I am the stepdad out of *Liar Liar* who tries to do 'the claw', I feel like the kids even give me a little pity laugh at times. Truthfully, the kids' games are quite shit and boring at times, so I get no enjoyment playing with them at all, as they tell me off the whole time. They are both very strict on the rules and how they wish it to be played, so I am very restricted with my character play. I would like my dinosaur to be stomping down the street, attacking people and knocking down the houses. I'm told by the kids that this is not how my dinosaur behaves, he is actually very placid and will just follow their dinosaur in the search for a spaceship that has landed close by. See how annoying this is? Like a dinosaur wouldn't even be able to fit into a spaceship!

I feel like I have got distracted ... back to Terry. Like I mentioned before, Terry struggled to recognise that Fin was autistic in the early days, and I did wonder if he would really ever get it like I do, but thankfully he does; it was just a long walk for him to get there. I think it can just be harder for the men sometimes, as typically they are not around kids as much. So, they don't have anything to compare to, and they also don't often have anyone they can talk to about it.

Even going to baby groups and school pick up, Terry has often told me he feels uncomfortable there, or that people don't talk to him. I mean, to be honest, this could be because he has a fuck off face, and nothing to do with him being a dad. He is just massively not approachable.

Out of the two of us, Terry is usually the strong one. He's the one who keeps it together when the rest of us are falling apart – except after having Poppy. Weirdly, it was Terry who crumbled this time, not so much myself. I think people forget that men can experience depression after a birth too, especially with how hard Poppy was in the beginning. It took him much longer than me to bond with her and stop being so afraid. I know he felt riddled with guilt about Fin being left out while we were always trying to comfort her. I can only hope I was as much of a support to him as he was to me in my darkest times, and we're pretty lucky we didn't experience depression at the same time. What a mess that would have been.

The best part of my day is always when Terry gets home from work. I can't tell you how much I look forward to it. Now, don't feel all fuzzy and warm inside reading this – I love him to bits, but this is not a romantic tale. It is more selfish reasons that I look forward to him being here. When he steps through the door, I feel instant relief. You see, I spend the day outnumbered, breaking up their fights but when Terry is here, it's two against two and we are bigger. Often, he will get in straight from work and go upstairs and run me a bath. He is very much a walking green flag.

I am often in awe of all the single parents out there, and the ones with useless partners. I truly think they're incredible, as I would struggle so much more without Terry. They say, 'Happy mum, happy family' and I really do believe this is true. In order for both parents to be happy, they also need a break at times. The most wonderful thing with Terry is that I don't even need to tell him. He doesn't need to hear me say it or beg for it to realise I need a break as it has been a tough day.

I am aware that Terry is going to read this book though, so I really need to balance this out before his head gets too big, so here is a list of all the things that he does to annoy me:

- Gulps loudly when eating toast (how I imagine a troll would swallow).

- He muddles mine and Poppy's clothes all the time when putting them back in the drawers.

- He leaves his giant work bag on the floor in the kitchen.

- He won't let me do the food shop at Aldi anymore as he says I can't be trusted (I'm sorry but the middle aisle calls to me, I have got some great stuff from there).

- Leading on to, he is very boring with money and expects us to do something called SAVE, rather than spend it.

- He falls asleep instantly in bed – I am completely jealous of this one. I feel it is because there is nothing going on in his head, which I just don't understand.

- He thinks me getting undressed for bed is a come on. It most certainly isn't. As well, as me bending over – again not a come on.

- He plays Dungeons and Dragons. This was hard to even admit. He plays it with his friends in the garage and it is very much a dirty little secret that we try to not talk about too much in case I get the ick. I think I would prefer him to head off to the garage to watch some porn, but no, I know what he is up to in there. Rolling the dice and . . . actually, that is all I know about DnD, and that is all I need to know.

. . . writing this list is really fun and therapeutic actually. I recommend this to anyone if your other half is pissing you off.

But I really would take all of these things any day over a husband/dad who didn't put his family first, and we have never come second to anything with him. I think that a marriage that stands through the test of children and especially children with additional needs shows how strong it is. We have nothing left most of the time for our partners, after days of trying to get them to school, trying to teach them to communicate, meltdowns during hair washing and getting dressed, taking them out and about to be judged by others, fighting the systems, fighting for financial support, fighting for a school place, waiting for a diagnosis and taking them to appointments, we are burned out. We have reached our limit and come the evening, we can barely even talk to another person. And our partners have to put up with this, it's not our fault but they must feel bottom of the list at times.

Sometimes, Terry has been back from work a few hours and I realise I haven't even asked him how his day was. I was so caught up in what the kids have been up to that I forgot about him.

I do feel bad in all honesty. I sometimes forget his needs because I am too focused on making sure everyone else's needs are met. He does at times go to the bottom of the list, even though he should be at the top (with the kids obviously).

It is all about compromise and adjustments, giving and taking. As long as you are both giving equally to your relationship and the kids, no one will end up feeling resentful. Apart from the sex side, I am pretty sure Terry feels resentful about that at times and has definitely muttered under his breath that the kids are cock blockers. We schedule it in like we do everything though – I find it a bit like going to the gym. I hate the thought of it and can't be arsed to, but then after I feel much better and think, 'Ah I needed that.'

Anyway, that's TMI I feel. If people want to know more, I will make a second book of that, titled *No Sex in the City* or possibly *Make It a Quick One, As I Want to Catch Up on My Programmes* . . . and they say romance is dead.

Top Tips

☆ *Try to go on date nights if you can, even if that means setting up a candlelit dinner in your lounge with no phones allowed.*

☆ *Make sure you both get a break from the kids at times. If you can't together, then do it separately.*

☆ *Schedule sex, otherwise, you may end up never doing it.*

☆ *Try to remember to check up on your partner, as we can sometimes get caught up in the life of kids. Check how their day was at work or how they are feeling.*

Chapter Seventeen

SURVIVING THE SCHOOL HOLIDAYS

Well, how do we start this one?

As I've reached this part of the book, our school holidays have just started here, which is why I am already a bottle down writing this. I just hope I make it through to see the finished published book. The six-week holidays are seriously a terrifying time. The first week is the kids being completely dysregulated and out of routine. The following weeks are spent trying to keep them entertained, usually contending with rubbish weather. Then comes the final week, full of meltdowns and anxiety about going back to school again. What a wonderful time, said no one ever!

I really don't remember my own school holidays being this long, but maybe it was because I was enjoying them. OK, I must put this out there before everyone thinks all I do is moan, it's not all bad. I do enjoy some days in the holidays. Some days we go out, have a lovely time, and I think, 'This is great.' However, there are a lot of days that I think, 'Have I died and been sent to hell?' But then I realise, no, even hell isn't this bad.

It's the constant eating, the constant whining and the constant making a mess that really sends me over the edge.

I really don't understand how they make it through school without eating basically a ten-course meal all before 10am because apparently when they are at home, they are wasting away if they can't eat whatever they desire as soon as they desire it.

How they are not 20 stone in weight from all the food I will never know. If I ate like that, I would probably be sick. And of course, they will still complain that there is no food in the house, even though the reason there is no food in the house is because they have bloody eaten it all.

Then there are the sibling arguments. The never-ending fights over absolute useless, irrelevant crap I don't give a shit about, and it goes on all summer. Some of their arguments are so bloody ridiculous that I think maybe they just enjoy fighting with each other. I will list for you some of the ridiculous rows they have had:

- One of them sat on the sofa too close to the other.

- One had more crisps in the pack than the other.

- One was humming too loudly/quietly/annoyingly.

- Who Frankie (the dog) loves more.

- Looking at each other too much.

- Playing with/touching/looking at a toy that they themselves have not so much as glanced at for at least a year.

- One of them chose 'elephant' as their favourite animal. This was the wrong answer.

I could carry on, but it will really bore you. In the end, I give up trying to referee this absolute bullshit. I figure they can just fight it out to the death. It's natural selection at this point and really, I shouldn't interfere with nature.

I couldn't intervene even if I wanted to anyway as I can't reach them through all the piles of shit on my floor. To be fair to Fin, this isn't caused by him. Fin sits on his tablet or switch and that's about it. He is past toys now, not that he ever really played with them much in the first place. He liked the idea of having toys, but he has always been much more technology focused. His imaginative play has never been great, I think because he is so literal with everything. It is in there; it just only has an outlet for certain things. The drawings he comes up with and his imagination when he is stimming take me by surprise.

Poppy, however, gets every single toy and object out to put around the house. We will often find an odd sock in a candle holder, or a coat hanger in with the bath toys. You absolutely cannot move these items or dare to throw them away either, even if it's an old wrapper or a stone. Fin brings the order, while Poppy brings the chaos, which can obviously cause clashes in their personalities. They will often set each other's meltdowns off, one covering their ears while the other is screaming. I feel like the holidays are just them tag teaming who is going to scream the most that day. It is very rare to have a day where we have two happy kids at the same time, unless they are in different parts of the country.

On the odd occasion though, they can sometimes work together. There was one time I was upstairs painting, and I made the biggest mistake any parent in history can make.

It was a rookie mistake, a schoolboy error.

I ignored the silence.

I know, I was stupid. Fin came up the stairs at one point though and said, 'We are making snow' and this, this was my second error.

I just replied, 'That's nice.' I was half listening and didn't consider what making snow would mean. When I got downstairs, I realised, with mounting horror, the folly of my arrogance.

I had left an open box in the lounge, full of polystyrene blocks from a large delivery. The box was now empty, but my lounge was not. It was everywhere. Under the sofa, on the table, in the drawers, under the TV. We were still finding the bits months later. For those struggling to understand think of a block of polystyrene, the kind that protects a TV inside the box. Each block is made up of millions of little polystyrene balls smooshed together. Imagine some-one un-smooshed them, all of them, and then tipped the result all over your whole life.

shudder

Poppy could literally make a mess out of anything though. I believe, she could honestly make a mess in a completely empty room, I am sure of it. She is usually the feral-looking child coming out of school with her hair all over the place, food all over her shirt and face, and grazed knees, whereas the other kids still look as they did when their parents left them that morning. Not to mention, she often has pen all over her face as she loves to draw on herself. I think this could be another PDA thing. The teacher tells her to draw on the paper, so what does she do? Draws on herself, of course. And my walls unfortunately, which is the reason why we have permanent markers hidden now.

The thing is, she loves drawing, so we do make sure we stock up on all arty things over the holidays and playdough. I know many people hate the stuff, but I find it really calming for my two. Plus, we have a laminate floor. Trust me, if we had carpet, I would not feel the same. It isn't just Poppy that makes a mess. Occasionally Fin does too, but where Poppy sets out to make a mess, Fin does so no less efficiently, but somehow completely by accident.

He squeezes the squish balls too much and they burst all over him. This has happened a few times now and once was in the car. I just stared at him, literally covered head to toe in slime, all stuck in his hair and over the car seats. It is amazing how much slime these things hold when popped. It looked like someone had just set off a load of slime bombs in the car.

But mess or not, sensory toys are an absolute must have in the holidays – scrap that – all the time. We have boxes of squishy balls, poppits, long stretchy things, squish pads, sensory tubes, fidget spinners. The fidget toys and colouring will only keep them going for so long though, soon we must venture out and we know that anywhere we go in the school holidays is going to be busy as hell. I honestly think this is the worst thing with the holidays, all the people everywhere, all the time. And it breaks my heart that our kids miss out on so much because they can't cope in such busy environments.

There is only one way we can tackle it and that is to head out at the crack of dawn, which is perfect in a way because any SEN sessions there are will usually be at around 8am or 9am. That's all we ever get offered, and we are somehow supposed to feel grateful for the fact they give us this tiny little timeslot when we all know they wouldn't make any money at that time anyway. Pah. They really think we are stupid.

The other way to get around avoiding the people is to head to the park when it's pouring with rain. Yep, it's not great fun but it is still better than the kids not going at all. I have spent too many times arriving at a park for the kids to take one look at it with all the other children running around and then refuse to go in. So, in the pouring rain we go, and we do the opposite on the hot days. On a boiling hot day, while everyone else is at the beach, we head to a stinking, sweaty soft play. It's not where I would choose to be, but the kids really don't do well in the heat anyway and the only way they would be truly happy would be to be in a swimming pool, but it is just pointless trying to go to an outdoor swimming pool on a hot day in England.

We did make this mistake the last school holidays and the queues were all the way through the car park. I went with some friends with autistic children too and we all said there is no way we could ever queue up as the kids would never cope, so my much more ballsy friend marched to the front of the queue and spoke to the reception asking what they were doing for autistic children and the response was nothing. We then had to leave, which is sadly the case too often, and something that really needs to change. Equality shouldn't just mean everyone gets what they're given, it should mean everyone gets what they need.

I really think, sometimes, we would be best off just moving to a deserted island somewhere away from people.

There are just too many people everywhere all the time. Even on bloody dog walks, I can't get any peace. I cross the road to avoid other dog walkers as I can't be arsed with the rubbish chit chat. Maybe we need to be more like dogs, scrap the small talk, just smell each other's areas and off we fuck... not so sure about that now I've said it out loud!

Sometimes you must brave the people though, otherwise you wouldn't get to go anywhere. We have braved the zoos, farms and theme parks if the places we go to offer carer tickets and ride access passes. Honestly, if they do not offer this, we don't go. I am not paying £100 for us to leave after 30 minutes because the kids can't cope with the crowds.

I will share a little secret I have with you all to make the day a bit better. I go around the places backwards – not literally walking backwards, that would be very weird. I mean starting at the end of the route, and heading to the beginning, even if it means you must carry your kids or get them in their buggies to run to the end point, to then start your journey. There is usually a path that people tend to follow around, so it means that you are likely to get a very empty area to yourself for at least an hour until people start coming.

Another thing we do in the holidays is compromise on days in and days out. We try to alternate the days so we will do the first day in, second day out, and so on. It helps us all as days out are so bloody overwhelming. Once we have had a big day out at a zoo, for example, it's nice to know that the next day we just say sod it and spend it in our PJs. The only thing that causes a problem with this is the dog walks. Frankie needs his outings, of course, but the kids don't want to go, therefore I end up doing something a bit mad but no surprise there.

I take the kids and the dog out in the car; we find a field to park up at, I give the kids their tablet computers and snacks, while I run around the field, or sometimes literally run around the car with the dog, still keeping my eye on them the whole time. These moments always make me laugh. I think of all the strange things that we SEN parents do, for an easy life!

I often think there is too much pressure on parents to take the kids out constantly during the holidays, and I think that social media, again, doesn't help with this. People are always filming their days out and their holidays, and it can make you feel like shit when you do nothing with the kids, but I have found that doing nothing is some of my kid's favourite days. They don't want to be out all the time; they just want to chill. I look back at when I was younger and we didn't go out every week, there just wasn't the options to for one thing. We didn't even have soft plays back in my day and a trip to the zoo would be for a big event like a birthday. You didn't just go there because it was a Saturday. So, remember to not be so hard on yourself if you have spent the week in with the kids, getting bored is OK for them. It means they learn to make up their own games. You could even get them to do some chores. I do this all the time with mine, which Fin hates. He will tell me he is bored, so I tell him he can do some chores. Yeah, not so bored now, are you?

I feel it is much like when you told your parents you were hungry, and they would offer you a fucking apple. I didn't say I was hungry for vitamins, Mother.

Don't judge me though, I am not all bad. I do offer them money to do the chores, which Fin will usually say yes to as he wants it for his games. Poppy though, cannot be bribed as you can imagine and is insulted that I would even suggest to her that she would do chores around the house like some kind of fucking peasant.

Because of the kids' moods, and their shifting idea of boredom, it is hard to plan days out in advance. I have booked so many trips before that we have had to cancel, as one of them is really dysregulated that day and can't cope with leaving the house. Booking things in advance usually makes the tickets cheaper, which is why I did it, but trust me, you end up losing so much money in the long run as you can't attend anyway. It is far better in my view to see how the kids are feeling that day and then go. Obviously, with autistic children this can be an issue if they like warning about things, so I try to prepare them anyway. I will say to them the night before that we are planning to go out the next day but try to be vague with where exactly in case that changes.

However much you try to plan for the holidays though, you need to accept some days will just be shit, possibly some weeks too, so get as much help as you can get. I know many of my friends have found personal assistants or carers to take their children on some days out. If you are offered this service, then use it. I have never applied because I know that my children would be absolutely terrified and not want to go. Another thing that I think can sometimes be more difficult with the in-between children, as they are more aware. They have the understanding that it is the school holidays and would completely guilt trip me that I was trying to get rid of them, the little fuckers.

I can't tell you the number of times I have been to Ikea and looked at that children's babysitting service they have there. What a bloody genius idea! Obviously not for SEN children though, as most of them would need a one-to-one support with them. The ironic thing about it though is we are the ones who probably need the babysitting service more than anyone else. Our kids are the ones most likely to kick off around the store and stop us from being able to shop!

I do get my help from Terry in the holidays though. I make him book off every Friday throughout the holidays just to break up my week a little bit. Not for us to have a lovely family day out or anything, no way – sod that. It is for me to just leave them all and go and mooch around the shops or sit in Costa for an hour enjoying the peace. Nothing fancy like a spa day (as lovely as that would be) but honestly, give me a shopping trip alone to The Range any day and I am as happy as a pig in shit. That day to yourself is so important, you start to feel your strength coming back again after the bastard's have spent the week grinding you down.

Sometimes we need to have these breaks to be the best mum we can be again. You imagine working solidly for 48 hours without a break and how poor you would start to get at that job from exhaustion. It is the same when being a parent, like the saying goes: you can't pour from an empty cup.

The one great thing about the holidays though is no school runs and no rushing around in the mornings, ironing uniform and packing lunches. Obviously, there will still be no lie ins, I don't think my kids have ever laid in. One time Poppy woke at seven, that's the closest we have got to it. Don't you love it when people say, 'Put them to bed later and they will get up later.' No, that is not how it works at all. Putting them to bed later means not only do I lose my evening, but my morning as well as they still wake up at the same sodding time, trust me.

I do think the school holidays get a little easier each year as the kids get older. I find myself feeling all emotional and upset when I hear those stupid guilt tripping posts on Instagram saying, 'Remember, you only have 18 summers with your children.' Fuck off! This doesn't help anyone. It doesn't force anyone to enjoy it anymore, it just makes them feel bloody guilty that they are not appreciating every moment. Nobody can possibly enjoy every moment of everything, it's just not possible – especially when it is an objectively miserable time.

You can be in the best relationship in the world and your partner will still get on your tits sometimes and that is the same as being a parent, it is literally impossible to appreciate every moment. Do I appreciate the cuddles I get? Yes. Do I appreciate them spitting my home-cooked food out? Do I fuck.

Look, I love spending time with my kids, but just not all the time and that is the problem with the school holidays. The same as my hubby and my friends – I love them to bits, but I really wouldn't want to be with them every waking moment. I think it is very easy for people to say they love the school holidays and can't understand parents who don't when they are the people that maybe have family that look after the kids or clubs they go to. We don't have that, so at least let me do something that I do enjoy doing, which is having a bloody good moan about it!

Top Tips

☆ *Don't feel pressure to do too many activities.*

☆ *Get your partner to book days off work, so you can have some days to yourself.*

☆ *Try to find SEN sessions in your area.*

☆ *Go to the parks on rainy days and soft plays on the hot days to avoid the crowds.*

☆ *Alternate days in and days out, so the kids don't get too overwhelmed.*

Chapter Eighteen

WE ARE ALL ALONE, TOGETHER

Life can be hard at times, and I use humour a lot to get through the dark days, as you will hopefully have found throughout this book. You can either cry about the really shit times or laugh about them, and sometimes I do both. I cry so hard I laugh, then I laugh so hard I pee. It's the circle of Mum life.

The harder days are getting less frequent as they get older. I say this just as we are about to head into the teen years and the hormone-fuelled hellscape of puberty, so I may need to retract this statement in book 2.

One thing that sadly doesn't get better and I feel gets worse in some ways is people's prejudice and judgement. People think that autism traits are quirky, funny and sweet when they are younger. A little toddler spinning in circles and chewing on their chew toys or dummies is adorable but unfortunately, a 14-year-old doing the same is not seen in the same way.

I have seen the stares that we get when Fin is having a meltdown. You can see it written on people's faces thinking that child is too old to be behaving that way!

I noticed a shift at mainstream school with the children also. The children that were so accepting when they were younger have become more ignorant with age, not all of them thankfully, but some. Kids can be so cruel with anyone different than the norm. It's funny because as a child you spend your whole life trying to be like everyone else, but when you are older you try your hardest to be different from the crowd. You realise that being different is an incredible quality to have. Who the fuck would want to be the same and boring like everyone else? But trying to teach our kids that just falls on deaf ears. And I get it because it did when my mum was telling me the same when I was younger. The only thing we can do as parents is to keep reminding them of how proud we are of them and how they should be proud to be autistic.

I do genuinely mean this too. I don't believe that autistic people have superpowers or are even all gifted, but I do believe the world is a better place with autistic people in it.

Overall, autistic people are honest. There is no manipulation, no fakeness and no filter at times and I really feel that I am a better person for having autistic children. I don't think I would be who I am today, without them showing me how the world is through their eyes. I wonder sometimes about the kind of person I would be without them. Would I be a judgy person? They have definitely taught me to never judge other parents for the decisions they make. Maybe I would have been someone that frowned upon a mother for giving their eight-year-old a dummy. I hope I wouldn't. I would like to say I wouldn't be but in all honesty I don't know. Unfortunately, it's not usually until you have walked in someone's shoes that you realise not to judge.

Our kids force us to stop and take in the things that

others ignore. We often must stop everything we are doing and watch an ant carrying a leaf to its home. I have grown to cherish these moments and see the wonder of this incredible world we live in that gets missed so often by being too busy doing shit that really doesn't matter. After watching the ant for some time, we then decide to build a home for the ants, so we have to research what they eat, what their home looks like and how many can live together. We then find books on ants to learn about their behaviour. While others are running around heading to the shops or soft plays, we are now experts in ants somehow and have learned to appreciate even the tiniest little creatures on our planet that others would simply not see and step on.

As much as there is beauty in autism, the struggles are so hard to watch. The hardest part of it is usually there is nothing that we can do to stop them having these struggles, we just have to make sure we are there for them for comfort, or sometimes as a punch bag. I know that all of us parents feel the exact same and that we would take these struggles away from them in a heartbeat if only we could. And that is something I have learned on this journey, and sadly had to accept. We can't fix the world for them; we can try to make it as best as we can, but in reality, our children are always going to have a tougher time in their life than neurotypicals.

I see our amazing kids trying to navigate this neurotypical world and I am so proud of every one of them. It sounds so strange to say that but I really do feel proud of everyone's children, as well as the parents fighting for them every step of the way. I am often in awe of my friends who have high-care-needs autistic children. I look at them raising their non-verbal children by communicating with them in so many ways other than speech. I have watched their children's eye contact grow, I clapped when seeing them point to something for the first time, and I cried with some of those mums when they finally heard their first word.

And with my fellow parents of low-care-needs children, I have watched my friends fight for their autistic girls to get a diagnosis, even though it is so often dismissed. I have seen their girls struggle at school and be told they are just rude, when their mum sobs to me knowing that no one understands their daughter like she does.

I watched my friends with their older autistic boys trying to cope with the teenage years and the hormones. At times I have seen my friends scared from the violent outbursts, but also watched the remorse I can see their child feels after.

I have also laughed with friends about things that no one can teach you about autism. Things that you have no clue as a parent how to deal with. Things like getting completely naked every time they need the toilet, kids grabbing our Tampax and using it as a chew toy and teens jerking off to Thomas the Tank Engine. You wouldn't find this information in the leaflets, but it's all part of life and it's nothing to be ashamed of.

Please don't forget that it has taken me a long time to get to where I am at now. As I said at the beginning of this book, I was very depressed and very lost when this journey started. Coming to terms with raising children with disabilities is not something that will happen overnight. You go through many stages of embracing this new life. Over time you understand your child's needs more. You learn to accept that things will always be different. You go through the stages of anger at how hard everything is and even begin understanding your own triggers.

It is so important to understand what triggers you because if you are stressed and overwhelmed, it will only add to your child's stress too. I have learned with time that some of my kid's verbal stims really trigger me, so I actually wear their ear defenders when I need to. Another one is when they use me as a climbing frame, so I now redirect them. You are allowed to not like things as much as they don't, so don't feel like you just have to put up with this as their parent.

When I say things have got easier for us, I don't believe it is because the children have changed, but it is because we have. Our outlook on life began to change. I meet with the teachers at school pick up every day, not to find out how well they did at Maths or English, but to find out if they were happy and played with any friends today. Your goals shift in life. You are not hoping for your child to win the sports day race, you are just hoping they take part. And no one will be cheering them on harder than we will.

I wondered for a long time if my kids even cared whether I was there or not. There are so many times they don't even acknowledge me when I get home from being out all day. I have to force them to hug me, and it can hurt at times. I start to wonder if they feel anything for me at all, other than the fact I am the provider of snacks and Wi-Fi. But then I remember every single school event I have been to; I see their little faces searching for me through the crowds and their face light up when they see me. It reminds me that they do want me there and they do love me even if they don't always know how to show it.

I have heard many parents with non-verbal children say that the one thing they long to hear the most is the words 'I love you' from their children and I completely get that. I can't imagine how hard it must be to never hear their little voices, or these words said to you. I have to say though, having verbal children doesn't always mean you will hear that either. My children have never said this to me first, ever. They repeat it back to me (sometimes) but usually after a lot of prompting. They have never randomly come over to tell me and I long to hear this too. The fact that I know they physically can say it, as they are verbal, can sometimes hurt more, as they choose not to. Well, at least that is what I thought for a long time. Now I realise that saying something such as 'I love you' could be as impossible for a verbal child than it could for a non-verbal one, as speech doesn't always mean communication. Communicating how they feel is one of the hardest things for my children to do, which is why they need emotion cards at school to help them express it. Expressing their love for me is still an emotion and like Fin has told me before, why should he need to say it when he already knows he feels it?

Trust me when I say, your kids love you more than anything in the world. Whether they can tell you this or not, I know they do. You are their safe person. I fully understand wanting to punch me when I say this by the way. The number of times I would be crying to people explaining Fin's horrific meltdowns at home and they would simply say, 'Ah, but you are his safe person.' That is fab,

I am pleased I am the safe person, but I would love it if he opened up this job role to a few more people, as it is fucking exhausting being the only safe person around here.

Anyway, whether you like it or not, you are home to them and their comfort and the one who knows them inside out. I know you want to hear those words but also feel it instead with their actions. (If you are going through a violent stage of them hitting you, you can just feel their love a lot more intensely than some.)

The thing that I love the most in the autism community is the fact it doesn't matter if your child is non-verbal with high-care needs, or verbal at a mainstream school – we all get it and know how tough it is. That is something I have found hard to accept in all honesty. At times I have worried that people would think I was a fraud talking about how tough it is to raise autistic children. I worried that the community of parents who have children with complex needs would look at me in disgust and say that I have no idea how hard it is, and I appreciate that I don't. I don't have to worry about things like when my child, if ever, will talk. I don't have to worry about my child hurting me or someone else (actually possibly with Poppy sometimes), and I don't have to worry about teaching them how to use an AAC device, but I do have my own worries still.

I worry about them being vulnerable and people taking advantage of them. I worry about how life will look for them when they are older. I worry that Poppy may never progress enough to get a job or get married. I worry that Fin's social anxiety will hold him back throughout his life. I worry that they may always need me, and that I won't always be here for them.

These worries though can eat you up if you let it. The reality is that none of us know the future, but the only thing we can do is ensure this generation does better than the last at looking after our most vulnerable. When it's my time to leave this world, I hope that if someone saw my kids, for example, struggling to pay at the shops, they would step in and help them. I know I always will. I will continue to watch out for the most vulnerable in our society as that could be one of my children one day.

When I began to build my social media pages, it made me feel less alone. I felt like I had found the modern-day village. There is a song that always resonates with me, it is for Trans rights I believe, but I relate to so many of the words.

'There's something wrong in the village, they stare in the village' and that is the reality of the actual village where we live. Many people don't want to form friendships with the 'weird' ones, the ones who are different. On social media though, the village is there. Thousands of miles apart from each other, but all living similar lives. The support of others who get it is the best thing about this journey, and a lonely place to be when surrounded by people who don't get it.

I have had well-meaning friends say to me before that their toddler is having a meltdown, so they understand how hard it is when, in fact, their toddler screamed for about two minutes because they didn't get the ice cream they wanted. No, that's just a tantrum. Very different, trust me.

People say to me they completely understand autism because their mum's best friend's uncle's wife had a daughter from a past relationship that was friends with the sister of someone with autism. Yep, you get it.

You then have the ones that tell you to not worry that your child didn't eat their dinner because their kid refused to eat a piece of broccoli once. Thank you for your help but my child has now not eaten her dinner for a week and is losing weight, so maybe take that piece of broccoli your kid didn't eat and shove it up in your fat gob to stop you talking such utter shite.

Seriously though, I know people (mostly) mean well and I know it is difficult when they sometimes don't know what to say when we are telling them we are having a tough time. I think the issue is that people always want to fix things, they need a reason and an answer to something, and our children are complex. There is no fix to some things, sometimes we just need to hear these words: 'I am so sorry you are having a shit time at the moment, here is some wine.'

And that is one of the reasons I really wanted to create this book. This isn't a miracle book that will give you answers to all the problems you face with raising autistic children. I wish it was, because I would be a millionaire right now, but instead it is the book that says, 'I see you and I hear you. I have been there too. This shit is hard, but you will get through it, because you always do.'

Raising autistic children is tough at times and it is totally fine to admit that, but the great thing is, the good outweighs the bad. People say that only special children are given to special parents, but this isn't true. We are simply ordinary people raising extraordinary little people, and what a gift this is to do.

Top Tips

☆ *Believe in yourself as you are stronger than you think.*

☆ *Stop worrying about the future, you can't predict what will happen and worrying will not change anything.*

☆ *Find comfort knowing that you are not alone.*

☆ *Find your village. Whether it is neighbours, friends or online. Ask others to support you, the way you support them.*

☆ *Be proud of how far you have come on a tough journey.*

BONUS CHAPTER:
THE GUILT GREMLIN

Hi, it's me again. You thought we were done but after the unprecedented success of the first edition of this book, many of you asked for an encore, so I couldn't just leave you hanging until the next book, could I?

It suddenly dawned on me that I had covered so much in this book but not really spoken about guilt. This seems crazy to me now as the guilt lives with me every day in some shape or form and definitely needed a chapter of its own. The fact the guilt lives with me every day could actually be the reason I *didn't* speak of it. When it is a consistent presence in your life, you stop noticing it – it just becomes the norm. But just because it is something we are accustomed to doesn't mean it is something we have to accept.

So, let's delve into mum-guilt starting with a time quite recently when we endured a traumatic three-hour car journey. This is another topic I haven't yet spoken about: the absolute hellishness of driving with kids. Or – even worse than driving – being stuck in traffic in a little box of hell with two screaming, moaning knobs, with no way to escape. What has this got to do with guilt you ask? Well, this car journey was us driving back from London zoo. This was a day out booked by me in a moment of panic and a pit of guilt that we hadn't done enough over half-term.

Were the kids upset we hadn't done enough? Of course not. Were they happy to sit around the house doing fuck-all for the week? Hell, yes! Did I listen to any of this? Nope.

If you ever want to experience being trapped in the car with kids (I have no idea why, unless you feel a need to punish yourself), then simply go to London during rush hour. Nothing will test your patience more than trying to navigate the awful London roads, taking ten hours to move one mile and the kids repeatedly asking when we are going to get there or shouting the dreaded words, 'I need a wee!'

It really doesn't matter if you make them go to the toilet before leaving. Trust me, 20 minutes in and they will need to go again. Of course they will, because the bottle of water you gave them was downed before you even left your street! Usually, getting them to drink takes bargaining and blackmailing, but not today. Why, you ask? Because they are arseholes.

I mentioned briefly earlier in the book about when they were young and stopping at traffic lights would cause the biggest meltdowns. This has got better as they have got older, however some things have got worse. For example, the little escape artists going Houdini on me while we are on the fucking motorway. They can't open a packet of crisps by themselves or tie their own shoelaces but if it comes to something horrifically dangerous that will make me look like a neglectful parent then, trust me, they will be able to do it with casual ease.

Poppy once managed to not only unstrap herself but

also the actual car seat from the car. Don't even ask me how – that thing was an absolute bitch to get in in the first place. She must have morphed into Stretch Armstrong. I joke, but in reality, it was terrifying. Especially as I only found out as the car came to an abrupt stop, causing Poppy's whole car seat, including her, to lurch forward into the back of the passenger seat. Luckily, she was fine. I, however, was not.

I was a mess, and completely riddled with guilt at what a careless monster I was. Mum-guilt is the one thing that continually rears its ugly head and I think this happens whether your kids are neurodivergent or not.

It lurks around in the shadows just waiting for you to fuck up and the second you do, it pounces. Reminding you of all the things you should have done better, whispering in your ear about what a piece of shit you are for letting your children down. Much like the voice in my head that tells me that 'it's only *one* more biscuit – go on, one never hurt anybody'. I know I should ignore it but, instead, I listen to it and now I'm five stone heavier and sobbing into my Hobnobs.

I think mum-guilt is often the result of all the bloody judgement around us. If you are a stay-at-home mum, you are called lazy and shiftless, and told you should get a job to provide for the family – why is it all on your husband? If you are a working mum and put your kids into childcare, you're neglectful – where's your nurturing spirit? Why did you even become a mother? If you are too hard on your kids, they won't have a good relationship with you, but if you baby them too much, they won't have a good relationship with anyone else. You literally can't win.

Let's be honest, we all fuck up sometimes. Especially with the poor first kids. Christ, they are made from tough stuff from all the times we accidently dropped them on their head or left the house without them, forgetting we even had a child. Look, I only did that once, OK? It was for about 30 seconds while walking to the car. It wasn't like I went off for a full day's shopping trip and then realised. Don't judge me!

One of the biggest mistakes I made was when Fin was a toddler. He was playing with money and enjoying putting the coins in his money pot over and over. While he was quiet, I went on a phone call. During this call I heard a gasping, choking sound and spun around to find Fin laying on the floor looking at me, desperately trying to breathe. I knew instantly that he had swallowed a coin and it was probably lodged in his throat. I then made my second biggest mistake and in sheer panic I shoved my hands in his mouth trying to find the coin to pull it out. Thankfully this worked and I got it, bringing a load of blood up with it from scraping his throat in the process. I now know that was the worst thing to do and I could have blocked his airways even more, but in that moment of terror, you don't think – you just react.

But over and over, I kept asking myself why on earth I would leave a toddler to play with money while I went on the phone. What kind of mother would do that? I now know the answer to that question. A fucking tired one. One that was trying her best and made a mistake because she is human. One that was learning, for the first time, how to look after a small hairless monkey with no sense of danger. One learning to cope with her first child in a situation where everything was new and difficult, as keeping a little person alive is actually quite hard work.

And don't get me wrong, even though Poppy was the second child, I still made mistakes with her too. One of them being leaving the front door unlocked quite often. The trouble was, I never had to worry about this with Fin. He was the child who followed the rules, the one who occasionally would put me on the naughty step because I needed to learn, so I got complacent. But Poppy proved to me you should never get too cocky as a parent. Don't worry, she never got very far, but it was always the thoughts of what *could* have happened that kept me up at night.

One moment of 'what could have happened' which made me sick to my stomach was the time I made the mistake of having a poo. I know – what a bloody awful neglectful mother I am to have the audacity of having a bodily function and abandoning my children like that. I am sure this is actually what goes through Poppy's head as she always feels the need to sit with me while I am mid-shit and tell me how awful the smell is and how I should be ashamed of myself, while also refusing to leave the room.

Anyway, I digress. I was mid-poop and there was a knock at the door. I ignored it and assumed they would come back ... but then I heard talking. With my knickers down by my ankles I crept out of the bathroom to the top of the stairs to find the door wide open and the postman there, being told about 'mummy doing a big poo'.

Oh, good.

'Just leave it there, thank you!' I shakily call down to him as I try to hide my vag hanging out, in case he decided to peep up the stairs. Thankfully, this is now just a funny story and embarrassment was the only consequence. But it did leave me thinking afterwards that it could have been anyone at the door talking to Poppy. In the pit of a bad nightmare the thought comes unbidden: they could have taken her. It honestly makes me feel sick to my stomach. It goes to show how incidents can happen so quickly, no matter how hard we try to be on top of everything as a parent. We all make mistakes and we all fuck up at times, but the important thing is for us to learn from them.

Having said this, if Terry ever makes these sorts of mistakes, I come down on him like a ton of bricks, poor sod. You see, it's a genuine mistake when I do it but if Terry does it, it is because he's an idiot. OK, don't hate me. I am joking . . . a little. It's the same when I shout at the kids. Sometimes I lose my shit. Trust me, I try my hardest to do gentle parenting but after the fiftieth time of saying, 'Don't do that', you don't feel very gentle anymore and sometimes shouting really is the only way that they bloody listen.

But only I am allowed to shout at them, no one else. That is the rule. If Terry shouts at them, I will go mad. I instantly start telling him off for scaring everyone. In reality, he is just doing the same as me. But, I don't know, maybe it's the lower voice – it just seems worse somehow. Like a moody troll bellowing around the house. Not to mention there is a part of me that is thinking, 'Why the fuck are you shouting at them? You have only been here an hour after work. I've had them all sodding day!' Having said that, they are experts in irritation and can be bloody annoying in a very short space of time.

One of the worst feelings of guilt was leaving Fin at school in the morning, screaming and begging for me to come back. That guilt walks around with you all day, no matter what you do or who you see. In the back of your head, you are thinking about that little face with their watery eyes wondering why you abandoned them. And it hurts. It really hurts, especially when you know they are in the wrong school setting. You are left with the fear all day of how they will be. Will anyone help them if they are distressed? Will anyone even know? The thought of it truly breaks your heart.

But you can't feel guilty for things that are out of your control. We all want the best for our kids and want them to be happy and we do whatever we can to make that happen. But we are limited in this world, especially in this neurotypical world not designed for our children.

Unfortunately, we can't always get the schooling that we need for our child. It's heartbreaking to accept this and it shouldn't be this way, but with the lack of funding from the government, many of our children will continue to be forced in mainstream school settings even when they are not appropriate for them. Coming to terms with this was soul destroying but there was never a reason that I should have felt guilty for this. It wasn't my fault and it is not your fault either.

As I have said before in previous chapters, this world isn't designed for our children, so everything through their lives is going to be that much harder for them. Which is not OK and it is unfair, but sadly it is the way it is. We can't spend every day riddled with guilt that they are not getting the support they need. The ones in power should be the only people feeling guilty about that.

All we can do is keep fighting, keep advocating and keep

teaching the world about our incredible kids. And for our kids, we can be the ones to support them and hold their hand through this life. Don't feel guilty, feel proud that you do this every day with no thanks for it.

Seriously, stop being so hard on yourself. Being a parent is hard. Being a SEN parent is unimaginably hard at times. It's like trying to swim from one side of the river to the other, except you realise you are swimming through thick mud ... while wearing a rucksack full of rocks ... while the person you are with is casually trying to drown you. That swim will be one of the hardest swims of your life and it may take you days, weeks or even years longer than others to reach the other side but, honestly, when you do, it is beyond worth it and you will appreciate it so much more that someone who just jumped in a boat and got there within an hour.

So stop being so hard on yourself. You are amazing.

Top Tips

☆ *Stop feeling guilty about things you can't control.*

☆ *Remember that we all make mistakes, but learning from them is the important thing.*

☆ *Be kinder to yourself; this is fucking hard work!*

☆ *Don't drive autistic kids around London ... ever. Unless their special interest is traffic!*

FINAL WORDS

And that, my friends, really is the end of the book. So many of you have contacted me or left reviews to tell me how you feel less alone since reading it and, to be honest, that was all I ever wanted from writing this. I am truly grateful to you for taking the time to reach out to me.

A SEN parent's journey can be a long, lonely road. Even when we are surrounded by people, we can feel completely isolated at times. We battle school systems, we fight for diagnoses and support, we comfort our children during meltdowns while trying to stick to their strict routines, we try to enlighten the world about masking while protecting our children from peoples' judgements and we do all of this while being your everyday 'normal' parent, partner and colleague. And that is why we need the village. And this right here is our village. Every single one of you reading this now is part of it. Whether we live five minutes down the road or 500 miles away, we are living different but very similar lives.

And maybe one day when our paths do cross, I will be there to pick up your shopping bag that you dropped because you're chasing your child across the road. Or maybe you will be the one who gives me your understanding smile when you see me comfort my child during a meltdown. And this community will be the one in the future who recognise when one of our now adult children is struggling and reach out to support them as if they were our own, if their own parent can't be there to do that.

So please remember, I see every single one of you and this is why I am so grateful to you for buying my book and being part of this incredible SEN community that we are continuing to build together, not only for our support now but also for us and our children in the future.

As strong as a mum

The reason they say
'As strong as a mum'
Is because you keep going,
Without help from anyone.

The chores still need doing,
Even on the darkest days,
The kids still need you
With a smile on your face.

You can't stop now,
Routines must remain,
And you can't cry for long –
You need to help with their game.

You're the maid, the referee,
The taxi, the cook,
And yet people still say to you
How tired you look.

You're supposed to work, be a mum,
Be a wife, do it all,
But who is there to catch you
When you eventually fall?

While picking up the pieces,
From your children, you hide
The pain you are in
And keep it inside.

It's true what they say –
This job's as hard as they come.
It's relentless and exhausting
When the work is never done.

But as tired as you are,
You never lose face,
Because you know that you are
Your children's safe place.

So, when you're feeling low
And say you're 'just' a mum,
Remember, to your little people,
You are the earth, the moon and the sun.

BONUS JOURNAL: YOUR DAILY GUIDE TO RAISING THE SEN-BETWEENERS WITHOUT FALLING APART

Who spends some days feeling completely stuck because you have a hundred jobs to do but no idea where the fuck to start?

Who spends their days trying to get the chores done but then feeling guilty for not spending enough time with the kids?

If so, welcome to your daily guide to help you navigate the times when you feel you are being pulled in lots of different directions, especially if you are neurodivergent yourself. Kids always come first with everything we do and this is usually because we are having to follow their strict routines and special interests. However, that doesn't mean we have to completely forget about ourselves in the process, or that all our other responsibilities conveniently go away.

I personally find it really hard to stay on task with anything. My house is often a mess, I am usually running late and my friends haven't heard from me in over a week. Now don't get me wrong, this guide isn't going to suddenly turn you into a PTA Pinterest mum – I can't work miracles, guys. But I hope it may help a little in feeling calmer and less stressed in your normal day.

On the following pages you'll find daily journal prompts for a week to help you prioritise. Yes, I know 'prioritise' is a horrible word that is usually only used by the knob-head manager you want to punch in the face, but prioritising will make a difference to how you feel and help you put in place some helpful habits. Now, let's run through some of the sections together. Trust me when I say none of this is a demand and this is not a guide where you must tick everything off the list. These are simply prompts for you to come back to in those 'stuck' moments we all have and the times we know we have tasks to do but can't seem to focus on getting one thing done. So, let's break it down, task by task

- **Time to stop what you're doing and do the boring playtime** Yes, playing with kids can be really fucking boring. It doesn't come easily to us all but I find it's good to give them some one-on-one time in the mornings on the days they're at home with me and soon after they return home on a school-day.

  Saying to them that you will play later doesn't mean a lot to kids when they have no concept of time, so they will likely harass you until you play anyway. If, however, your child doesn't enjoy playing with you, still try to make time for some interaction with them. You could try some sensory play or some 'bucket time' (putting different objects in a bucket for them to pull out, touch and look at). Tick this off when complete and then you won't feel so guilty for ignoring them for the next hour while you clean.

- **Speed clean** Set a timer for an hour or however long you have and speed clean – clean as if someone is popping round to inspect your house. I would recommend putting on your favourite music and cleaning as much as you can in each song before it comes to an end. Yes, you may be doing this with a little one hanging off your leg but give them a mop and let them 'help'.

- **Break time** TAKE A BREAK! Make a cuppa and sit down. Treat it as a break at work. Try your best to get some you-time. Throw whatever you need to at the kids so they will leave you alone for ten minutes. Seriously, this task is just as important as the rest. You cannot pour from an empty cup.

- **Easy wins** This is time for you to tackle the odd jobs; put a wash on, take the bin out, check the school emails and prepare the dinner (which for me means checking we have enough nuggets in the freezer!).

- **Prepping for the next day** To make the next morning easier for you, prep tonight. Get the uniforms ready and ironed. (Do people still iron? I am always told they don't but I am obviously showing my age as I still do!) Get the lunches packed (as much as you can). Even getting the car keys ready by the door can help. If getting the kids ready in the mornings takes you a couple of hours, the last thing you need is to be searching around the house for the bloody car keys when you are already late. Check their school bags! Make sure everything they need is in there.

Most importantly – have you got enough milk for your morning coffee? There is literally nothing worse than finding out you've run out when you have been rudely awoken at 5am to a hyper child forcing you to get up.

- **Mini journal of your child** I know the last thing you want to do once the kids are finally asleep is to sit down and start writing but I can't tell you how much this will help you. Not only will this help with any future appointments as evidence but also for you.

  You don't have to write an essay – just try to note down any meltdowns or signs of regression, but don't forget to write about the small wins too! Over the days you may spot patterns that help you understand possible causes to your child's behaviour this week.

- **Be proud of yourself** Fill out this section of the journal with your achievements. Some days go to shit. Don't beat yourself up about it. But do recognise the things you have achieved today, no matter how small. Even if it is getting out of bed. You did it. Tomorrow is a new day.

DAILY PLANNER

Here we go again ...

M T W T F S S

Time for the boring playtime! ☐

Easy wins
Put a wash on ☐
Prepare the dinner ☐
Take the bin out ☐
Write your shopping list ☐
Check the school emails ☐
Load the dishwasher ☐

Prepping for the next day
Get the uniforms and your clothes ready ☐
Pack as much of the lunches as you can ☐
Check school bags ☐
Check fridge ☐
Check keys are ready to go ☐

Be proud of yourself
What have you achieved today? (No matter how small.)

Speed clean
Which room are you speed-cleaning today?

Break time ☐

Mini journal of your child
Happy moments and 'fucking hell' moments ...

Daily Reminder
Go text your friends and family back ... they have been waiting to hear from you and are getting more pissed off. Do it now!

__Well done!__ Now go put your feet up and chill.

DAILY PLANNER

Time for the boring playtime! ☐

Speed clean
Which room are you speed-cleaning today?

Easy wins
Put a wash on ☐
Prepare the dinner ☐
Take the bin out ☐
Write your shopping list ☐
Check the school emails ☐
Load the dishwasher ☐

Break time ☐

Mini journal of your child
Happy moments and 'fucking hell' moments ...

Prepping for the next day
Get the uniforms and your clothes ready ☐
Pack as much of the lunches as you can ☐
Check school bags ☐
Check fridge ☐
Check keys are ready to go ☐

Be proud of yourself
What have you achieved today? (No matter how small.)

Daily Reminder
Get your washing out of the machine. It's been sitting there a while and you know you will only end up washing it again!

Well done! Now go put your feet up and chill.

DAILY PLANNER

Here we go again ...

M T [W] T F S S

Time for the boring playtime! ☐

Easy wins

Put a wash on ☐
Prepare the dinner ☐
Take the bin out ☐
Write your shopping list ☐
Check the school emails ☐
Load the dishwasher ☐

Prepping for the next day

Get the uniforms and your clothes ready ☐

Pack as much of the lunches as you can ☐

Check school bags ☐
Check fridge ☐
Check keys are ready to go ☐

Be proud of yourself

What have you achieved today? (No matter how small.)

Speed clean

Which room are you speed-cleaning today?

Break time ☐

Mini journal of your child

Happy moments and 'fucking hell' moments ...

Daily Reminder

Sort through your post, especially those dreaded DLA forms. Don't keep putting them off. Grab a cuppa and go through them.

Well done! Now go put your feet up and chill.

DAILY PLANNER

Here we go again ...

M T W **T** F S S

Time for the boring playtime! ☐

Easy wins

Put a wash on ☐
Prepare the dinner ☐
Take the bin out ☐
Write your shopping list ☐
Check the school emails ☐
Load the dishwasher ☐

Prepping for the next day

Get the uniforms and your clothes ready ☐

Pack as much of the lunches as you can ☐

Check school bags ☐
Check fridge ☐
Check keys are ready to go ☐

Be proud of yourself

What have you achieved today? (No matter how small.)

Speed clean

Which room are you speed-cleaning today?

Break time ☐

Mini journal of your child

Happy moments and 'fucking hell' moments ...

Daily Reminder

Check through your emails and delete any you don't need. Same with all your photos clogging up your phone.

__Well done!__ Now go put your feet up and chill.

DAILY PLANNER

Here we go again ...

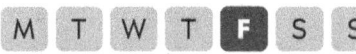

M T W T **F** S S

Time for the boring playtime! ☐

Easy wins
Put a wash on ☐
Prepare the dinner ☐
Take the bin out ☐
Write your shopping list ☐
Check the school emails ☐
Load the dishwasher ☐

Prepping for the next day
Get the uniforms and your clothes ready ☐
Pack as much of the lunches as you can ☐
Check school bags ☐
Check fridge ☐
Check keys are ready to go ☐

Be proud of yourself
What have you achieved today?
(No matter how small.)

Speed clean
Which room are you speed-cleaning today?

Break time ☐

Mini journal of your child
Happy moments and 'fucking hell' moments ...

Daily Reminder
It's Friday so check the kids' lunchboxes and don't leave them sitting all weekend in their bag.

Well done! Now go put your feet up and chill.

DAILY PLANNER

Time for the boring playtime! ☐

Easy wins

Put a wash on ☐
Prepare the dinner ☐
Take the bin out ☐
Write your shopping list ☐
Check the school emails ☐
Load the dishwasher ☐

Prepping for the next day

Get the uniforms and your clothes ready ☐
Pack as much of the lunches as you can ☐
Check school bags ☐
Check fridge ☐
Check keys are ready to go ☐

Be proud of yourself

What have you achieved today? (No matter how small.)

Speed clean

Which room are you speed-cleaning today?

Break time ☐

Mini journal of your child

Happy moments and 'fucking hell' moments ...

Daily Reminder

Check your calendar and whose birthdays are coming up. Go and buy a load of birthday cards and keep them in the house ready.

Well done! Now go put your feet up and chill.

DAILY PLANNER

Time for the boring playtime! ☐

Easy wins

- Put a wash on ☐
- Prepare the dinner ☐
- Take the bin out ☐
- Write your shopping list ☐
- Check the school emails ☐
- Load the dishwasher ☐

Prepping for the next day

- Get the uniforms and your clothes ready ☐
- Pack as much of the lunches as you can ☐
- Check school bags ☐
- Check fridge ☐
- Check keys are ready to go ☐

Be proud of yourself

What have you achieved today? (No matter how small.)

Speed clean

Which room are you speed-cleaning today?

Break time ☐

Mini journal of your child

Happy moments and 'fucking hell' moments ...

Daily Reminder

Fill up the car with petrol. Yes, I know you love running it on empty and seeing how far you can make it but, seriously, go fill it up!

Well done! Now go put your feet up and chill.

Acknowledgements

This bit I have probably found the hardest as I am terrified that I will leave people out and offend them, so it's probably going to end up including my postman, the ladies at the nail salon and my lovely neighbour, Wendy.

But in order to not make this book 3,000 pages long, I will stick to the nearest and dearest.

Firstly, to the most amazing lady who made all of this happen . . . El. Thank you so much for your constant encouragement in the times I've been saying, 'I can't do this, I'm rubbish.' Thank you for working tirelessly on this, the same as you did with the SEND Reform book. You are truly an inspiration.

To my incredible SEND Reform girls, you know who you are. You have been there through some of the toughest times. While we felt that other things were falling apart, we stood strong together. You are always there for me, even when I call you all up raging about something or rambling on with a two-hour voice note, and yes, while having a pee. I love you guys so much.

Of course, a huge thank you goes to my mum and dad. The ones I would call up crying down the phone to at the beginning of my journey, the times I was in a pit of depression, and you would come and pick up the baby for me to give me a break. And as you supported me as a carer to the kids, it's time for me to support you, Mum, as a carer to my dad, who has Parkinson's and dementia. I am constantly in awe of all you do and can still laugh on the darkest days. Love you both to the moon and back.

And I couldn't not mention my brother. Someone who I see so much of Fin in. Someone who struggled throughout school life, with no support and spent a lifetime masking. I am so proud of you, Jordan.

Another thank you goes to my amazing friends, Sophie and Hayley. Special people come into our lives at different stages, and I know you both came into my life for a reason. You both got me through the toddler years and became mine and the kids' safe place and for that, I will always be grateful.

My cousin Rachel, who is actually like a sister to me. Annoying and tells me off all the time (like not getting her Janet Jackson tickets). But in all seriousness, we have a bond like no other and still cry with laughter each time we are together. I couldn't have done this without your support and fighting off the trolls.

Another big thank you goes to my amazing hubby who really is my best friend. He puts up with me during my meltdowns and has taken over everything while I have been writing this book, while I still moan that he's done it wrong. The most amazing husband and dad to our kids. Love you.

And, of course, the biggest thank you goes to my amazing kids. I am hoping one day you will get to read this and know that despite the roller coaster we had along the way, I would always choose you both and never change you for the world. You both inspire and amaze me every day and don't let anything hold you back. Fin and Pops, you deserve the world, and I hope one day I can give it to you.